McCormick's

Guide to Staying Alive
in New Zealand

McCormick's

Guide to Staying Alive in New Zealand

Gary McCormick

Hodder Moa Beckett

Dedication

To Bruce Morrison, William Grieve and all the members of "The Crew". With thanks for all the good times we have had exploring New Zealand.

ISBN 1-86958-696-4

© 1998 Original text – Piano Productions
The moral rights of the author have been asserted

© 1998 Design and format – Hodder Moa Beckett Publishers Limited

Published in 1998 by Hodder Moa Beckett Publishers Limited,
[a member of the Hodder Headline Group]
4 Whetu Place, Mairangi Bay, Auckland, New Zealand

Produced and designed by Hodder Moa Beckett Publishers Ltd
Colour Separation Microdot, Auckland.
Printed by Kyodo Printing Co. Ltd, Singapore

Acknowledgements

Thanks to the many people who supplied photographs for this book:
Morrison Grieves, special thanks to Yvette Thomas and Bruce Morrison
Shelley Hanley
The New Zealand Herald
McCormick Private Collection
Sally Tagg
Peter Bush collection
Television New Zealand Publicity department

Contents

Foreword

It's become quite bloody obvious that the country

faces a dilemma. We've lost our way.

We need to look no further than the fact that Dame Susan Devoy became a Dame because (presumably) of her services to squash. I don't want to get offside with Dame Susan who is, as far as I am able to see, a very fine person in every regard. (I once got offside with one of the rowing sisters and she started calling me "Dr Death". These people are not to be trifled with.)

Nor have I read everything there is to read about Lange's "qualified privilege" legal proceedings. I have tuned in to Sir Geoffrey Palmer talking about the subject on National Radio, which makes me feel like I've lived through all the British and American defamation cases, not to mention Sir Geoffrey's own astute writings on the subject. But I feel that I am qualified to say (without malice, and Susan is a public figure) that squash is nothing to bother the Queen about.

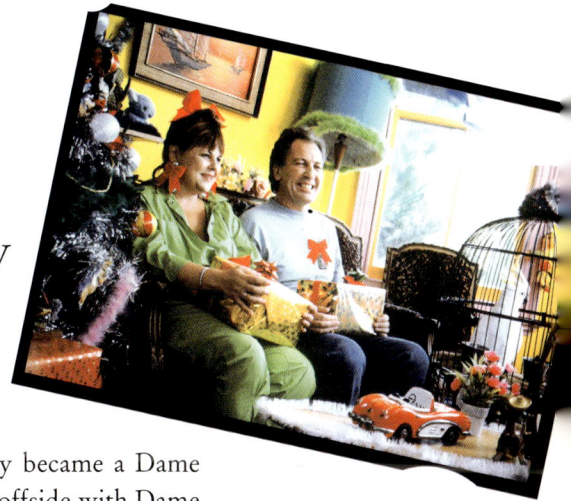

I don't know who sends these nominations in (National Party hacks, I suppose) but can you imagine Her Majesty opening her mail with a delicate gold letter-opener over breakfast and groaning every time she sees a New Zealand stamp? (If they are using those stamps with the ugly insects on them, she probably ran screaming from the room.)

Prince Philip has to go and find her.

"What do they want from me this time?" she says.

Of course they send out the Damehood because she's got no choice but to respect the view of "Her Majesty's Government" in the colonies, but at the end of the day Elizabeth II must be one of the most ardent supporters of a republic downunder.

If you've read the previous lines, you will know the country is in trouble. Not a single sentence makes any sense. Squash, or Squat, as Her Majesty probably calls it, is about batting a ball against a wall in a concrete cell.

Her Majesty is a queen somewhere in England.

Dame Susan has won a world championship four times.

I am not the king of England.

The same weekend in 1998 that Susan received her honour, the front page of the *Dominion* carried a colour photo of Ginger Spice, whose real name you did not care to know is Geri Halliwell. She was the ugliest of the five, who looked rather like Cilla Black without the stupid grin. Anyone could tell she was going to be trouble. I saw the film. She left the band, even though it's going to cause huge problems with the lip-synching, but the important thing is all the girls said they still loved one another even though they have to find another spice. (How about Old Spice – a hoary old bloke with hair coming out his nostrils and his ears, who, while the girls are dancing, stands up the back and scratches his arse?)

But why on the front page of a national newspaper at a time when we are facing Prebble-mania?? The country, politically speaking, has been a charisma-free zone for several centuries (apart from Michael Joseph Savage, who knew how to sit still long enough for a good black and white photo. He knew that Labour supporters would never put a colour photo over the fridge because it would clash with their lives!)

We flirted with Winston Peters and the Maori Worriers but, at the end of the day, wrap-around sunglasses start to look like white suits. You can bring back a stage musical of Saturday Night Fever as the English have done, but Election Night Fever only lasts as long as lunch the next day.

You need something more.

It's come to my **attention** that people want more than the mere mechanics of power.

The current crop of political leaders are tragically limited by their own experience.

Imagine being in a caucus for ACT, the Labour Party, NZ First, United (you'd be lonely), National or the Alliance. You'd rather be in the Legalise Marijuana caucus – even if you didn't like dope! Because at least they would be floating off remembering Led Zeppelin riffs. They'd be having a life – even if they were imagining it.

The time is dangerously close when people are going to want something to feed their political, social and spiritual hunger.

This book may be the single most important book ever written to sum up an age. Then again, it may not. But I think it will be.

Nothing in these pages will resemble the dry, crusty old sheets of paper which have been the analyses and manifestos of our past. On the contrary, what I have to put before you here are observations and impressions of people and places which reek of life. They come at you from life's kitchen.

I'm a televison star. I know what it's like.

ng There —
Poems
Work

CHAPTER 1

There can be no better time and place to write a book than Wellington in winter. Wellington, with its windswept streets and bars, is part of a new central region tourism marketing strategy to be known as Centre Stage. It is also the setting for Sam Hunt's poem "Early Opener":

A long-bar heater just above head height
burns your eyes until they smart
your forehead sweat,
makes your heartbeat rise like vomit.

There are enough old buildings in Wellington to make a slightly used and shopworn person feel at home. Stained and cracked concrete, broken footpaths and narrow streets assist the inward journey.

Writers are a personality type. Leo, Scorpio, Libra, Writer. They are the kind of people who end up down the back of the picture theatre, behind the tall person and the woman in a hat, ducking and weaving in a silent, crazed attempt to get a good view.

Always a little bit behind the game. Keeping up with the normal tasks and preoccupations in life, but with a sense of resignation that it will all end rather badly. They survive on the moderate amount of pain and humiliation the mildly retarded feel in the mainstream classroom.

If you recognise this feeling of dislocation, it's time you found the most conducive environment in which to write.

Auckland is a busy place and hours have to be set aside at traffic lights practising your road rage. (Police have suggested that we develop a non-verbal means of conveying regret to drivers we offend. One driver in South Auckland attempted it, raising his outstretched palms — and lost three teeth as a result. What he should have done is climb out of the car, roll on his back on the road, with his arms and legs in the air.)

Life in Auckland happens mostly in bars identified only by their initials: SUCK, POUT and BITCH. You must remember names (your own), where you last met, your last film project, etc etc. There is simply not the time to write it all down!

You may one day hear yourself saying to someone cute and thin, "Well . . . it's really much more important to live than it is to write."

Christchurch has the proud heritage of the Fairburns and the Glovers who struck out from the blinding, stifling English traditions to found a New Zealand literature — but even they, after a time, beat a retreat. I have a personal difficulty with trying to write in the City of Romance because A.K. (Alan) Grant lives there.

Alan is the kind of man you would call an "old friend" even if you first met him earlier that day. That's what I like about Christchurch and that's what I like about Alan.

A barrister, a wordsmith, a writer for *McPhail and Gadsby*, *Letter to Blanchy*, the author of numerous articles, columns and books, Alan is the sort of person you want to go to lunch with armed with nothing more than the intention of having a good time and saying goodbye to June (the month not the woman . . . although if you are having an affair with June and wish to end it, I suggest you go out to lunch with Alan and do both at the same time!).

In fact, to do justice to Alan – and to ourselves – we should all have written into our employment contracts an "A.K. Lunch Day" – a public holiday to be taken at will (or when Alan is available).

It's not often you get the opportunity to pay tribute to a living, breathing human being you admire. Alan is a writer and as such gets fired at him the arrows of unwarranted criticism. He, David McPhail and Jon Gadsby have been the backbone of successful humour in New Zealand for many years. They have afforded more enjoyment and satisfaction than any other team of television writers and performers.

It is an offence in New Zealand to be around too long. In some parts of the world, longevity is celebrated.

Ah, this is but a small area of quicksand through which we must make our way. We are a young country, a nation of people still unsure who or what to honour as taonga.

McPhail and Gadsby was not around long this year. Despite being a top-rating programme, it was cancelled after one short series, leaving the lads jobless.

I was once a liberal in many areas. I grew up in a state housing area where everyone had, it seemed to me, more than their fair share of problems. I therefore found it difficult to blame anyone. It seemed we were the victims of outside forces. Kids who were treated badly would obviously grow up and strike back. It was not their fault, or so it seemed to me at the time.

A.K. (Alan) Grant: The kind of man you would call an "old friend" even if you first met him earlier that day.

My attitude changed when the people of South Auckland allowed the Mongrel Mob to stage a "convention" in Mangere. In the course of it, members of the Mob picked up a young girl, put her in a van and gang-raped her for hours.

My liberal sentiments changed immediately. I went on National Radio and suggested a quarry be established where those convicted of the crime could dig forever. I mentioned this to Tim Shadbolt (another well-known liberal) at a hotel while we were discussing a "Great Debate" tour. He felt that the offenders should be shot — but that in endorsing such a penalty one had to be prepared to carry out the sentence oneself. We both felt we could do it.

In a further refinement, I suggested a legal point system for offenders:

2 points for trespass.
2 points for carrying a weapon.
2 points for using it.
3 points if victims are more than five years older than yourself (the bullying factor).
3 points for sexual violation.

Anything over six points and you have ten years inside – no questions asked. Over nine and you have twelve years (no parole). If you kill, then you leap to a base sixteen points before other factors are taken into account – twenty-two years, no parole. And if you reach twenty-five points, then it's thirty years (no parole) regardless.

The judges will have an easy ride.

The clerk of the court can do the sums.

Alan Duff: a brave stirrer.

I had turned from being the product of my youth into someone who feels that a line does have to be drawn in the sand.

Alan Duff is known as something of a hard-liner. He draws lines in the sand all over the beach!

Alan's achievement as a writer was to pass on to us another underground language and culture in *Once Were Warriors*.

At a function in Hastings for his marvellous "books in homes" campaign, he was being questioned about how he had the ideas for characters like Jake the Muss. He looked at me helplessly as if to say, "These people think I made this up!"

Some people see Alan as an outspoken "stirrer" playing into the hands of Pakeha who feel that there are "hand-outs" for Maori. In fact, he is brave enough to raise issues which must be talked through. We need more like him.

Alan plays golf, flies a helicopter, fraternises with wine-growers and creative people living a wonderful lifestyle in Havelock North, is married to a non-Maori and is building a magnificent Ian Athfield-designed house.

He is all of the contradictions, strengths and weaknesses we might hope for in someone who is able to give voice to a sizable part of the population hitherto ignored or who featured in our lives as crime statistics.

But back to Christchurch . . .

Alan Grant has good reason not to be my friend. On one occasion, during a celebrity debate in New Plymouth, I mischievously abandoned my teammates Jim Hopkins and Alan Grant and joined the opposing team – who were quite clearly going to win in front of a large, very parochial crowd. As it then became a debate of four speakers against two, the Taranaki team won easily.

When I got back from celebrating with the local team, it took a long time to explain to Jim and Alan how appropriate it was for me to be on the winning side. I still don't think they trust me.

My patience with Alan has been put to the test. Travelling south of Kaikoura in a van with Grant and Hopkins, I noticed a tiny movement on the railway tracks some 80 metres to our right. I was bothered enough by it to insist that we turn off the highway at the next opportunity and go back and investigate. It turned out to be a baby crawling down the railway tracks. (True!)

The child had **crawled** away from a nearby farmhouse and we were able to return the child to a **distraught** mother.

I expect no praise for this, but was somewhat surprised to see, three weeks later, in Alan's column in the *Listener*, a parody in which Alan recounted what had happened and then claimed that

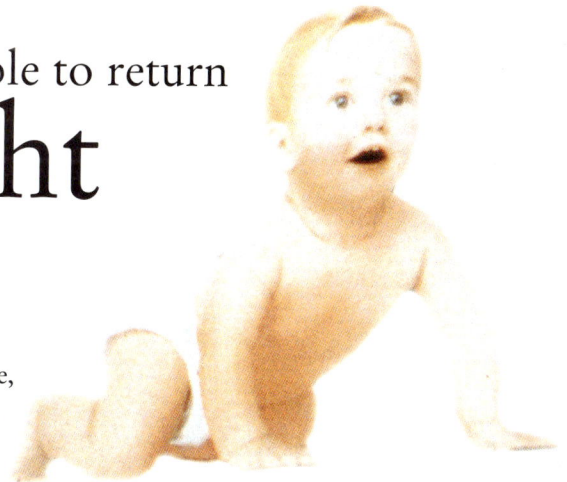

his superb eyesight enabled him to save many soldiers during World War I, when he used his biplane to lead a platoon back to safety from behind enemy lines.

(I could tell you a few things about Jim Hopkins too, but he always beats me in debates because of his final summations which are usually brilliant. The less said about him the better, other than that while touring with him he insists on taking in the "sights" – which usually means the Moeraki Boulders. It is excruciatingly boring, although I see they have now built an information centre about the little round rocks!)

I would call Alan Grant a friend even if he chose not to call me one. Why? Because if Alan said to me that he would not call me a friend, I would phone him immediately.

"Is that A.K. Grant?" I would ask.

"I think so," Alan would reply.

"What's this about your not being my friend?" I would say. "Let's talk about it over lunch."

We would then both be enormously happy and look forward to lunch.

sean Duffy has played a cop so often he thinks he is one.

Sean Duffy, the actor and director-person of *McCormick* and, among other things, the controversial "Wainuiomata: Beyond Nappy Valley" episode of *Heartland*, has actually offered to be my friend because, as he says, I am much too busy being self-absorbed and advancing my own career to have any friends. Sean has offered to be my friend even if I ignore him.

The barely masked criticism of my "self-absorbed" temperament is a bit strong coming from an actor. (Sean was a powerful presence in *Mortimer's Patch and Plainclothes*, as well as the mightily clever (and therefore under-exposed) comedy, *Neighbourhood Network*.

Sean is a male actor, coming complete with male hormones like testosterone and is therefore quite different from the women of the species, who are (I will mention some later) generous and sensitive to a fault. Male actors like Sean are very much of the "look at me, look at me – I'm an only child!" school of acting. As a result, they can be very embarrassing at parties.

Nonetheless, Sean's offer of a meaningless friendship is a very generous one. I have more or less taken it up (although I have not spoken to him about it because it would defeat the purpose). Sean is from Mt Albert, a suburb of Auckland where everyone (even small children) wears tracksuit pants.

Friendship among the people of Mt Albert is a kind of mutual taste-defence pact. There is a tacit agreement not to wear real trousers.

Dunedin is a melancholy, introverted city (with a controversial and brave Mayor, Sukhi Turner), populated by poets and musicians who favour the "Dunedin sound".

Writers in Dunedin very seldom leave (with the notable exception of Roger Hall). This may in large part be because of the many beautiful young women learning to be doctors and dentists there. I am troubled by this southern quicksand effect. Hardly a day goes by in Dunedin when a poet does not declare that he or she intends to move north – which he or she never does.

So Wellington it is. I grew up 25 kilometres to the northwest of Wellington, in Titahi Bay, the subject of a television documentary screened in March 1998. *The Bay Boys* was something of a catharsis. Early books of poems, notably *Poems for the Red Engine*, which put me on the road with Sam Hunt, were written about growing up in an atmosphere of not-so-polite menace.

> *The firemen set about*
> *lighting fires*
> *under chairs,*
> *breaking down doors*
> *pushing people around with their big hats.*
> *The ladies (some of them) were carried screaming*
> *down the stairs*
> *and some went willingly.*

> — *"Firemen's Balls"*
> *from* **"Poems for the Red Engine".**

This will be dealt with in greater detail in the next chapter.

It is hard enough to survive adolescence anywhere but all the more difficult in the shifting sands of a working-class community where people seemed to get old and hardened before their time. Where to fit in? How to belong?

We went to the Boys Brigades, Boy Scouts and Bible Class. The BBs, BSs and BCs were supposed to be fun and teach us about teamwork, leadership and other important things. I couldn't see it. Scout halls, community halls — people giving orders, whispy stubble on baby-bum cheeks, pencil-type moustaches throwing their weight around!

The scoutmaster, who was a bus driver in real life, had to be addressed as Akela, I seem to recall. I couldn't bring myself to say it. There was a lot of quibbling over chores. A hierarchy. Someone with a bigger penknife than me.

I wasn't a child genius at primary school.

I was okay at English, couldn't play the recorder, and I found that the answer to the maths was at the back of the grey exercise book. A girl called Carol always seemed to know what to do without cheating. It was obvious I was never going to beat her but luckily I looked in her Post Office book with the squirrel on the front and discovered she had £100 in there. She was an only child and rich.

Following a brilliant career as a house captain, chairman of the

Preparing to be precocious, the author is in the back row, third from left.

23

student council and head boy at Mana College, I went to Victoria University to study law. (Years later, the inspirational Mike Bungay QC acted for me in a case against a truck driver whose truck spun out on a road, running over a car I was driving and killing my girlfriend, Diane Columbus. I was very nearly moved to study it again.)

The law course at Victoria was way beyond a Bay Boy's dreams. I was smart enough, but I didn't feel at home with all those city kids. I perfected the six-minute run to the railway station. I would leave the lecture at five to the hour and be on the electric unit to Porirua at five past the hour. Which meant I could be in the howling nor-wester surf at the Bay an hour after that.

I got into **politics**, being elected to the Porirua City Council by one vote after the Labour Party insisted on a magisterial recount.

(I was elected as a so-called Independent.) The only reason I got in at all (then the youngest city councillor in New Zealand) was my determination in running dances and campaigning for a youth centre for people my own age, in a community which had virtually no entertainment facilities at all.

I sat through meeting after dull (and quite often vicious) meeting alongside the only two liberal councillors: the late, great, former All Black captain Ken Gray and Helen Smith, one of the most successful of the fledgling Values Party candidates (and still a wonderfully positive political force in the Porirua community). They were bleak meetings, involving two major warring factions. The current Mayor of Porirua and trenchant critic of *The Bay Boys* documentary, John ("it has set the city back twenty years") Burke, was a young Labour councillor at the time. He stayed. I left.

I did not see out the full term. I abandoned my responsibilities. I had to, because if I had stayed I would have died there. Fortunately the human spirit has a way of forcing the issue.

I went to Auckland at the time of the Cook Street market, the Gluepot, big crowds for the bands and the Indian summer of hippiedom which inspired love poems like:

I will remember
tall hills at Muriwai;
walking rain-drenched grasses.

A kind of love-stained glory
in those brush-broken skies: you did appear
in white and yellow then,

honest as the very flowers
that soften daylight;
as gentle by night
as ever I remember peace to be.

— "I Remember You as Peace and Broken Skies",
from **Naked and Nameless**

The music scene in Wellington was really lively in those days. I would walk (run!) from the Western Park Tavern in Tinakori Rd, down to the "1860" where Roger Fox (another Bay Boy) played with his big band; on to the Romney Arms where Simon Morris, Dave Feehan and crew played; the Southern Cross to hear Midge Marsden. All of this movement achieved in oversize fur boots which seemed to be all the rage (to me, anyway). If you knew somebody, you could drink late in the upstairs bar of the St George with Denis Mason.

The days of candles and incense have gone now. The ruthless eighties and the privatised nineties put paid to them. It is a source of wonder that poems go on being written (they are rarely performed).

Our poetry seems to be in the deft use of figures. Our Bible is the Reserve Bank Act. There is little or no generosity. No room for wonder. We are becoming a nation of cost accountants. As Sam Hunt had the prescience to say in a poem published in 1971:

> *So you may be a member of the act*
> *He makes for you your special coloured hat.*
> *Beware! He's fitting you for more than that.*

> — *"Beware the Man", Sam Hunt,* **Collected Poems,** *Penguin.*

We are all being fitted for more than that.

Sam Hunt and Minstrel strode the streets of Wellington and around the Paremata harbour.

> *It's said that children should not use*
> *stick figures when they draw!*

> — *"School Policy on Stickmen", Sam Hunt,*
> **Bracken Country,** *1971.*

Sam taught at Mana College for part of a year. A couple of years after that I approached his boathouse rather apprehensively, to ask his advice about my own poems. There on a drainage pipe a few yards offshore was the famous barber's chair. It was a salutary experience to be able to talk with someone whose life was so different. Which made so much sense. A man who was living the word.

I felt an enormous sense of joy following our short conversation. The words of another of Sam's poems, "Gaugin Through Fever", ran through my mind as I walked back across the inlet:

The mud shines, pock-marked after rain.
The tide is on an inward run.
Cockle-shells floating on its back . . .

That was the beginning of my new life. A determination to get the words out. To make sense of it.

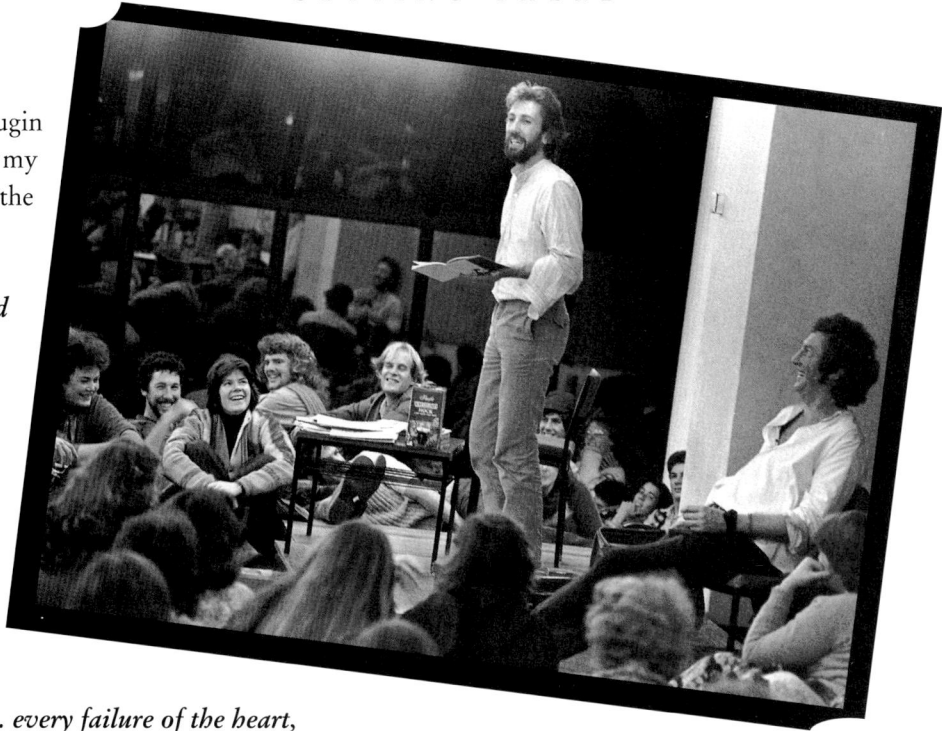

Sam Hunt inspired me to live the word.

. . . every failure of the heart,
every debt was paid for.
When next morning
I caught the bus to Castlecliff,
standing naked amongst the dunes,
nothing of the boy remained.
That is how we die —
let no one tell you
death comes once.
It comes a thousand times.

— *"Return to Kaiaua", from* **Zephyr.**

The Edge Town

ot

CHAPTER **2**

I have always been fascinated by people who are "different". Children can be fairly hard on other childen who are different and some people appear marked as the "odd one out" from a very early age.

What then can it have been like for Barry De Geest, one of six New Zealand thalidomide victims, born without arms?

I was delighted to learn from him that in Oamaru, where he grew up, people were kind and helpful. His contemporaries organised all kinds of games and activities involving him, including his role as coxswain for the local rowing team. Today he is the manager of CCS Manawatu. What an enormous amount of charm and humour Barry has!

The *McCormick* crew accompanied him and his staff to a recreational game of petanque (a game the French invented to make drinking in daylight hours easier to justify). It is a game he very rarely loses because – as you will have noticed if you saw the episode – he kicks the boule to a more advantageous position when he thinks no one is looking.

Even more wonderful is his delightfully outrageous claim that he should be allowed to win because he is disabled!

Some weeks later, I met a ski instructor from Ohakune who had taken Barry skiing. Because of Barry's disabilities, he can only fall directly forwards or back. This in itself would be problematic and painful enough to deter most people. Not Barry! He saw the day out, complaining only that the boots severely chafed high up on his inner thigh. He is an accomplished humorist and was the main source of entertainment in the apres ski bar.

Chloe Reeves: a rose in anyone's language.

Chloe Reeves, formally of Wainuiomata, currently of the Hutt Valley, is a standout of another kind. To put the record straight, we "discovered" Chloe by accident in Wainuiomata. We don't go out of our way on the *Heartland* programme to "discover" people. It was just that one of the crew saw Chloe and her scooter parked outside the local shopping mall.

She appeared to us (by virtue of her sense of colour – pink scooter, blonde hair) to be bright and cheerful on a rather grim mid-winter's day.

We were right. She is.

She had another asset from a television point of view: a great sense of delivery and timing. Given that you could not create a Chloe even if you tried, for she is 100 per cent the genuine article that you see and hear, it was an enormous bonus to discover that she intuitively understood how to "flirt" with the camera and signal her intentions ahead of time so that cameras were trained and at the ready.

We chased her on her way to her daughter's school, filming all the way.

We then followed them home to where her then partner, a motorcycle enthusiast of some description, was making up a railway track for his model train set.

Chloe, as she herself would put it, has not been "lucky in love", although her current partner, whom I met at the opening of Te Papa, appears to be a very considerate man. But our introduction to the bikie with the train set was memorable because while we were hastily introducing him to the film crew as we followed Chloe into the house, he

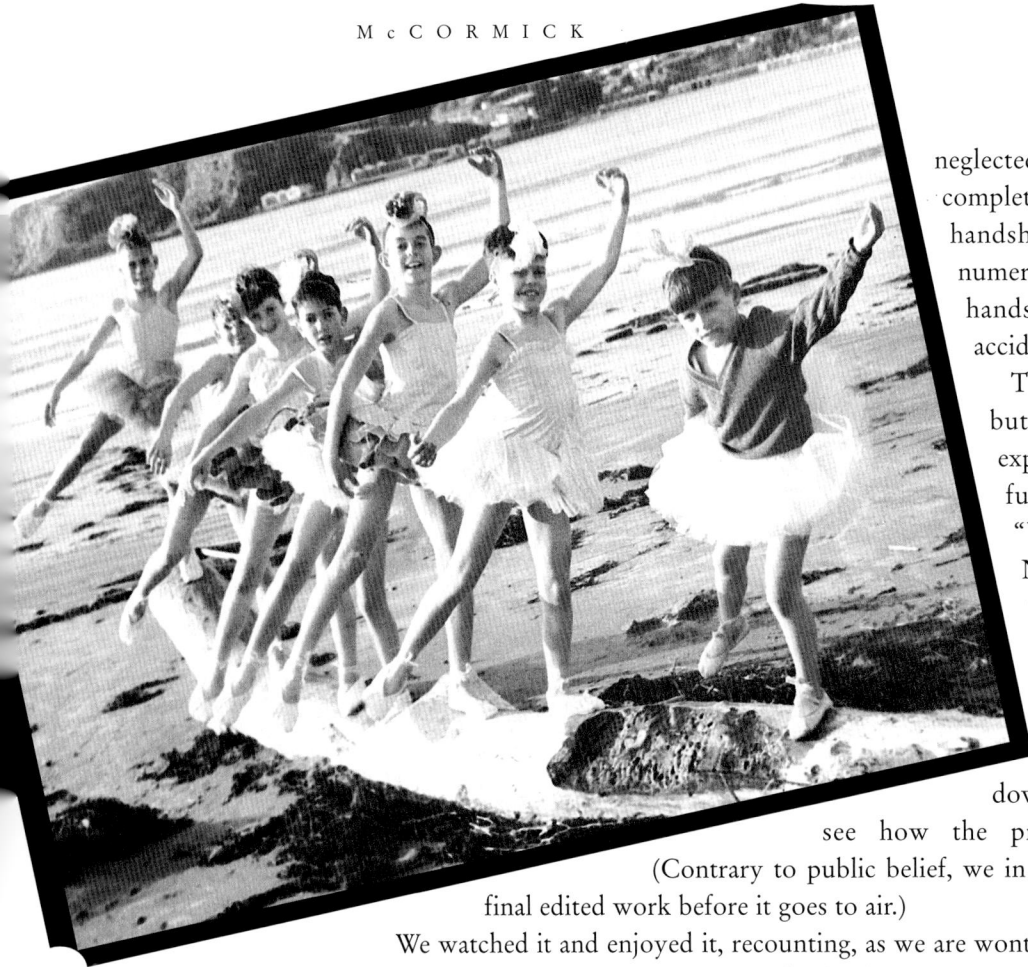

Early experiments in modern ballet on Tiraki Bay beach, the author is fourth from front.

neglected to mention until the completion of a round of hearty handshakes that he had numerous broken bones in his hands as the result of an accident.

The rest was pure theatre but not theatre that we expected would provoke a furious response. When "Wainuiomata: Beyond Nappy Valley" screened, we were on a filming expedition in the Far North and the publican kindly agreed to bring his own television set down to the bar so we could see how the programme turned out. (Contrary to public belief, we in the crew seldom see the final edited work before it goes to air.)

We watched it and enjoyed it, recounting, as we are wont to do, stories behind the stories (eg, the director drinking vodka back in a Lower Hutt motel and Cossack dancing into the wardrobe where he was found some hours later). Then the phone began to ring.

It kept on ringing all night long as outrage and indignation from Wainui residents spilled into newspapers, radio stations, MPs and Television New Zealand.

The gist of the complaints seemed to revolve around the male strippers (who take regular trips to Wainuiomata for "girls nights out"), Chloe and what was seen as a general putdown of "Nappy Valley".

The complaints came not from league club supporters but from the more middle-class members of the community who felt that they had been part of a move to elevate Wainui from its working-class roots – only to have their good work reversed by our programme. Property values were mentioned frequently.

The Hutt Labour MP, Trevor Mallard, sniffing a lynch mob in the making, offered to debate me – an offer which I accepted. We made the arrangements but he changed his mind, saying that he thought things were "getting out of hand". Someone in Parliament described Chloe as a "lunatic", which upset me greatly.

This fuss and the later one over *The Bay Boys* (in a sense, the West Coast's "Nappy Valley") highlighted three things:

I have been in dozens of arguments since then about the Wainuiomata programme. Most of them begin with groups of young men from Wainui approaching me in a bar to

- The loyalty we Kiwis have for our own turf.
- The difference between propaganda and documentary-making, which still confuses people.
- A rather unfortunate tendency to personalise these arguments, so that Chloe, for example, is vilified by those who did not like the programme.

tell me that they "come from Wainui". (There's no answer to that so I just shrug.)

The more disappointing ones are the ones in which people who appear a little more sophisticated introduce themselves and then launch into an attack on Chloe. This still happens – years later. I mount a fairly impatient defence and it almost invariably becomes obvious that the critic is a disgruntled person in their own lives. The unhappiness is not about Chloe, but about some personal disappointment, perhaps that they have not risen to public notice whereas someone like Chloe has.

I am not above pointing out where the real problems lie.

Aren't we all a little weird? My early memories of growing up in Titahi Bay are of wearing a Batman costume and daring to be seen from a distance by local boys who were much tougher than me. I think I thought that by suddenly appearing out of the

The author gets to sit on the principal's right. One of his brothers, Paul, is fourth from right, row 2; future sister-in-law Dori, fourth from right, front row; younger brother and current manager Mark reported as absent. Nepotism reigns!

bush as Batman, I could make a stand for public decency, law and order and not be recognised.

The *Bay Boys* documentary showed that there were two worlds – Porirua East, the wild state housing area, and Titahi Bay, also a state housing area but where sand and surf ameliorated the conditions.

The beauty of the beach (any beach) is that you have space to take your dreams away.

On Sunday evenings, Dunbar Sloane senior would return to the boat ramp at the northern end of the beach and give away tarakihi and snapper to those who wanted them. The clubbies struck out to sea in their surfboats and skis night and morning and the entrance to the Bay waited there like an exit door to the beyond.

When you live on a beach, you can turn your back on what you don't like of home, work, school.

Not long after *Bay Boys* was broadcast, I received a letter from a former (and very influential in my life) deputy principal at Mana College, Bruce Crowley, who still lives in Titahi Bay. It was he who encouraged my interest in English and, along with Edna Tait (later a president of the PPTA), my enthusiasm for debating.

In his letter he said that I reminded him of a story he heard about Mussolini's son. As the story goes, young Mussolini was part of a regiment marching past his father, Il Duce, when a lieutenant remarked to Mussolini that his son was out of step.

"Nonsense," replied Il Duce, "he is the only one marching in step." Allowing for the fact that I doubt anyone would have dared to tell Mussolini about any of his son's shortcomings on the parade ground, the implication of the story appeared to be that somehow I have a different or peculiar memory of what growing up in Porirua or Titahi Bay was like, that my experience perhaps did not correspond with that of my contemporaries.

About the same time, the Mayor of Porirua, John Burke, made a claim that *Bay Boys* had put back the city's image twenty years.

Had I got it that wrong? Porirua was not Bosnia.

There was only one moment
of intense agony,
when the fire station began to play
its giant harp
and the sand whipped up
while all eyes turned to examine
the sky
for tell-tale signs of smoke.
And the young men who shived one
another
at parties with flick-knives,
who were dangerous and sullen
and walked the streets in packs,
would suddenly become
model citizens, and climb aboard

the big, red engine
as if they were going to meet God.

As they swung out onto the road
past the old people
and their Chevies with the engines
still running
bleeding black and red sorrow
on the beach road
into the horizon,
we young boys trembled
and waited,
knowing our turn
would one day come
to climb aboard and disappear.

"The Boys" (a little bit older now) and the boatsheds, south end of the Bay.

"Knowing our turn would one day come to climb aboard and disappear."

Perhaps the "bodgies", as they were then known, looked a lot fiercer than they were. They were a continual haunting presence. When my friends and I saw them coming up the main road we would head down a sidestreet or cross the road and walk with our eyes down.

One of them was the son of the local mayor. He threw a rock from a cliff top down onto a gathering of officials (including his father) at the opening of a boat ramp. It struck a visiting dignitary on the head and he had to be taken to hospital.

The local volunteer fire brigade had its fair share of arsonists.

Ours was an island which was not an island. The causeway ran from Porirua, then still in the process of development as a ghetto, to the sea. A very narrow island it seemed too.

There were honest fights, like the one at the picture theatre (a former mess hall left behind by American Marines and now the Porirua-Titahi Bay Little Theatre) when bodgie gang members exercised their normal right to step to the front of the queue when the door opened for the five o'clocks. Old man Dolden, then in his fifties (which seemed old to us!) offered to sort matters out with gang members in the boxing ring at the nearby gym.

They agreed and we all left the pictures to gather inside there.

One of the bodgies stepped into the ring and the two fought it out, the result declared an honourable draw.

The social climate changed for the worse with the introduction of hundreds, then thousands, of migrant workers from the South Pacific, along with increasingly disaffected young Maori from Hawke's Bay and the Bay of Plenty.

The Bay Boys covered those difficult times. Tensions began to increase at Mana College in about 1968, a year in which I spent the first few months at a school in St Ives, north of Sydney. I was coming into my own as a surfer. Surfing itself was going through a renaissance: American long boards, the Beach Boys and Gidget were out. Short boards and the Australian animal was in!

The author as a lean, mean, 17-year-old surfer — Titahi Bay.

I arrived in Sydney as surfing was taking off as a statement of Australian nationalism. I got to hang around North Narrabeen beach – home of the surfing brave! I was stoked!

My Sydney college was posh. The boys wore long trousers and the young women were fabulously sophisticated. They wore makeup. I was the only person in shorts.

I had the misfortune to be billeted with a Christian Science family. I know very little about the philosophy of Christian Science and care even less. The household was dominated by an atmosphere of anxiety and oppression, mother being an overbearing, sanctimonious bully, whose aim it was to reduce her son Richard, my fellow Rotary exchange student, to a tiny, blinking replica of her sad husband. This she had largely succeeded in doing.

I did manage to develop my taste in practical jokes while in Sydney. One joyful evening I warned my fellow surfing campers at North Narrabeen that I was prone to sleepwalking (pointing out that sleepwalkers should not be disturbed for fear of doing them psychological damage). Thus insured, I walked around the tent for fifteen or twenty minutes later that night, kicking, standing on them and even eating the only cake we had in front of them.

I met my first eccentric genius – Richard Liney – at St Ives College. He was a brilliant, multilingual student who defied all attempts to make him turn out for physical education. This was tantamount to treason in Australia at a time when a man's goal was to reveal the cut of his genitals in Speedos and to captain a surfboat.

I supported Richard because I did not like coercion. (I felt obliged to turn out for rugby games which wasn't too bad because I was in the First XV at Mana.) This resulted in the two of us being hounded by the PE teacher, who had no idea that from his too-tight shorts to his leathery tan he was a caricature. On one occasion, Richard told him he was a caricature but he mistook it for "character" and went away mildly pleased.

More often than not, it became a very **unpleasant battle** between the forces of **prejudice** and the flame of originality.

When pushed, Richard would speak only foreign languages (he spoke four fluently) for days at a time.

Current Porirua
Mongrel Mob boss.

From this rather upmarket and intellectual environment, I returned to Mana College in the second term, my Christian Science Rotary exchange student in tow. On the first morning, as we stood making notes on our class schedules, a fight broke out between one Pakeha, twenty or so Maori and the same number of Samoans. The Samoans were a lot older than the rest – and bigger. The fight was vicious and resulted in some severe injuries.

My exchange student friend wanted to go home immediately and I wasn't that sure about staying on myself! For the remainder of the term, prefects toured in groups, teachers in twos or threes, and police patrolled the playing fields. Brawls were frequent and nasty.

A couple of years later I started running dances in Porirua and met George Harris (not his real surname by the way) and the makings of the Porirua Mongrel Mob.

I started the dances because with a group of kids calling themselves the Porirua Youth Movement we decided we weren't getting a fair deal. There was nothing to do. Bands were easy enough to come by and we could lease the Porirua Community Hall every Friday night.

I met George fairly early on, when someone explained to me that he was the "kingpin" (the best fighter) around Porirua. George didn't hang around the town centre like the others and I knew something about his family being strict (but I didn't know what that meant).

There was a dance at the Paremata Boating Club. You had to have a ticket to get in and supper was provided. I had a ticket because of my connections with a young woman who used to swear and abuse me when I crewed for her (a story which nearly sent Russell Coutts to sleep on a *McCormick* programme, but which I still think is bloody interesting!)

George and three or four of his mates had tickets too. They got in and were perfectly

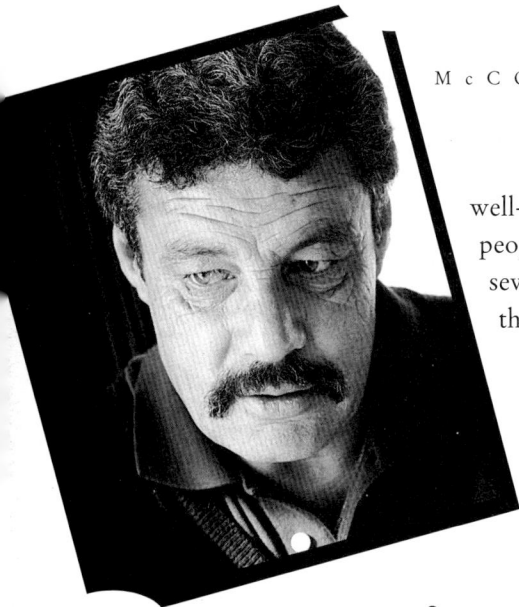

well-behaved. But the committee decided that they were not the kind of people required and a move was made to evict them. George was only seventeen at the time and a number of mature boaties moved in to see to it that George and his mates left.

George exploded.

He stood in the centre of the room **spinning in circles,** punching all and sundry to the ground.

George, the man who made it!

No one was able to lay a hand on him. To complete the job, he turned over tables groaning under the weight of well-prepared food. He and his mates left.

Five minutes later, he came back in again alone, as weeping, bleeding boaties were surveying the damage. He was under the impression that one of his friends was still trapped inside (which was not the case). I had overheard the club captain calling the police and, as George was quite clearly ready for more trouble, I stepped up to him, placed my hands on his shoulders (a terrible mistake!) and quietly suggested that now might be a good time to get away.

He sized me up and threw his head forward in a Liverpool kiss, but in such a manner as to deliver a glancing blow. I took it as a warning. It was a valuable lesson about mana and dignity on the edge of town. By touching him, I had put him in a position where he had to react.

It was never mentioned again and every Friday night George would turn up to help run the dances. This was the lad who had escaped over a dozen times from boys' homes, once within two minutes of being admitted. This was the boy who would walk back over the hills from Levin to Porirua during the night and wait until his father had gone to work, so that he could see his mother. Gang members and other would-bes used to travel from all over the country to fight him at the dances. He would be back minutes later and I never saw any blood on him (he used to wear white shirts).

As a kid, George was beaten, kicked and punched through the first floor window of the family home (landing on the clothesline below – which probably saved his life) by his father. He lived secretly on the clay floor of the basement of the family home for several years. My parents took him in from time to time.

He now has a wonderful wife and a family of high achievers. During the filming of *Bay Boys*, George had some misgivings (partly as the result of pressure from other branches of the whanau) about making the story public. I argued that it was a story which needed to be told and that in my opinion George (and, for that matter, his family) were heroes all. We had some disagreements and I saw the George of old rise up at the kitchen table, fists clenched, eyes burning. It was enough to remind me of the fear we all lived with.

So I don't think that, like Mussolini's son, I was out of step over Porirua. I was there – outside the hall on Friday nights, out of my depth. Watching Black Power pull up further down the road, the cops further up the road.

Everyone waiting for their chance.

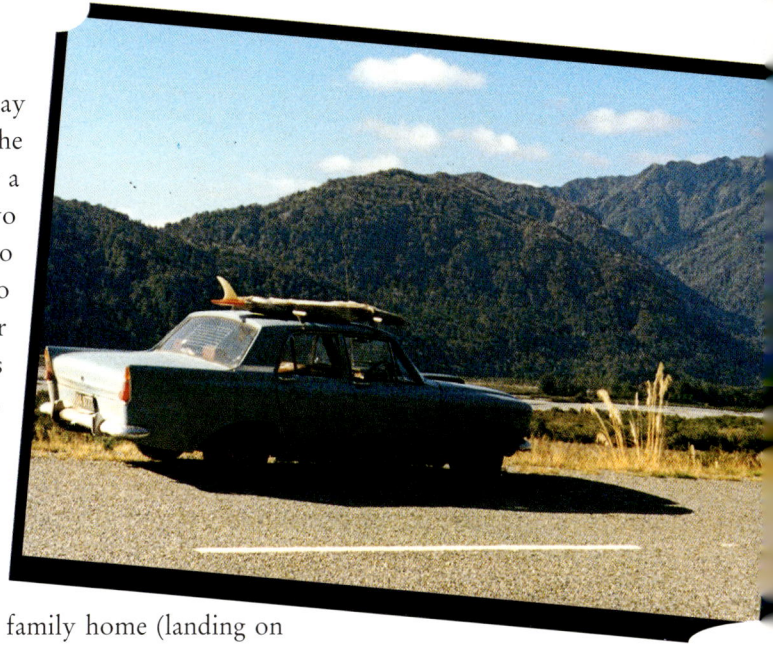

Have board, will travel: I travelled extensively in this car during tours with Sam Hunt.

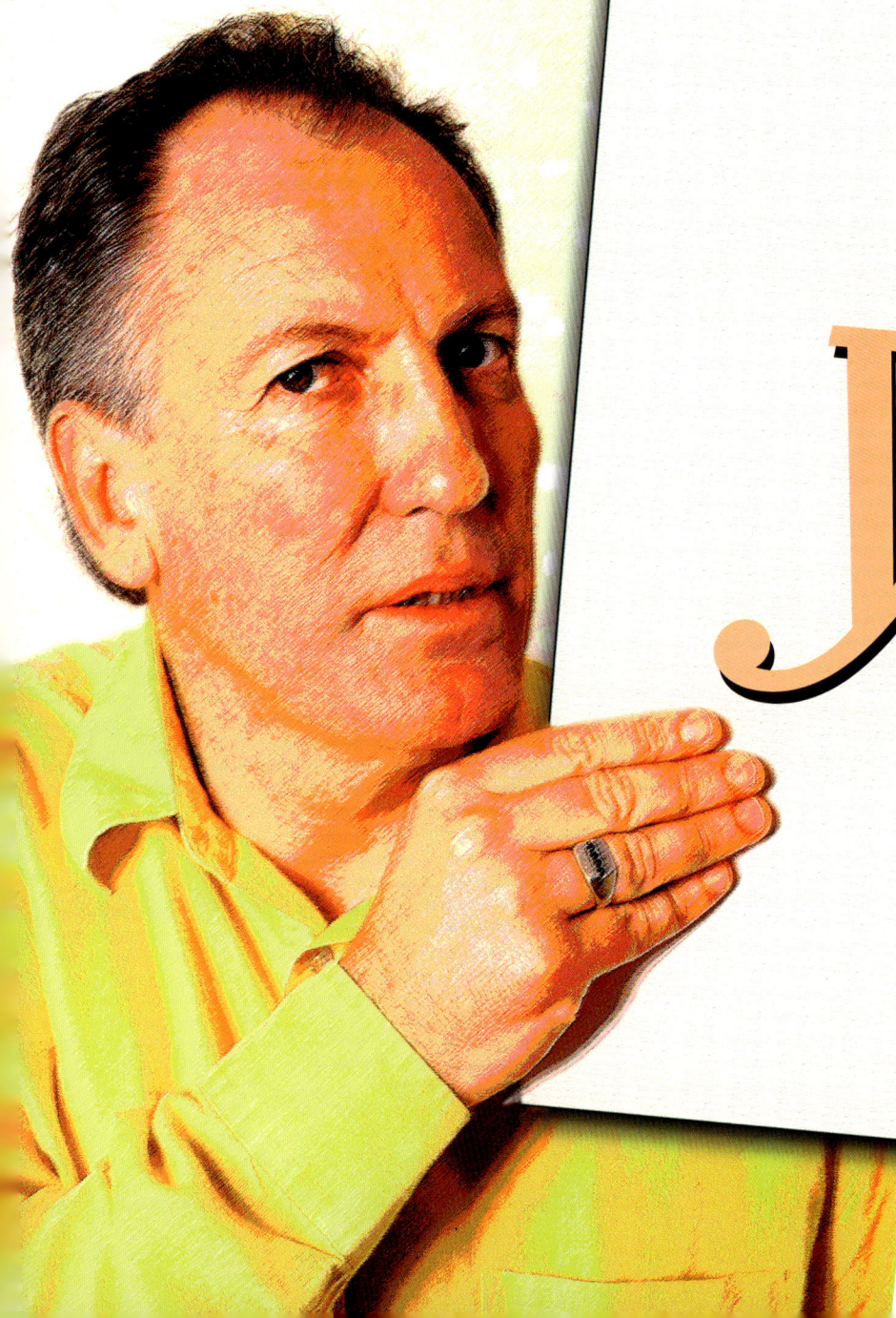

so
you

Why Were Born?

CHAPTER 3

Tragically and self-evidently,

you were born to die. A lot of modern books gloss over this. There have been huge numbers of self-improvement books published in recent times, all of which (if I may sum up) aim to open up the pores in your skin and make you more intelligent than you are.

Imagine if any of these books actually lived up to their claims. If you ate and slept and lived a sensible life in the manner laid down, you would be a great big, sterile, gaping pore!

When you were cremated, there would be no smoke. We wouldn't know if you had gone. The conversation would soon move on to Mr and Mrs Blackhead, who are much more interesting people.

This is the kind of mistake that people in the land of glistening pores make. They think that being a pore unto themselves is a worthwhile goal.

This is why all of those people in gymnasiums pedal on bikes which aren't moving. They don't know that they are stationary. No one should tell them. All that sad puffing and panting denotes a fairly deranged mental state. Their bodies apparently produce some kind of opiate which feeds on its own addiction. They are on a "high" – which is apparently about the same level (by our standards) as the lower rung of a bar stool.

There is no easy way to wean them off this internal homebake (unless there is insufficient ventilation, as so often is the case with uncertified laboratories, in which case they explode and lycra goes everywhere).

Human beings will do whatever it takes to get "out of it".

You cannot deter exercise freaks because punishment is part of the reward. The British medical journal the *Lancet* has published a paper showing that men who ride on the modern, hard bicycle seat for six years will become impotent (in which case they will take Viagra and never dismount). These men are laying their testicles on the line in order to remain thin, willowy (stick-insect scrawny) because they want to get laid! Which won't happen because women hate it when they tear their pantyhose against a snag (sensitive new age git)!

They will deny that they want to get laid because it is in their interest to do so. Because they can't.

Of all the sports in the world there are to think about, I like orienteering. (I like to think about badminton too, because everyone who plays it is called Roger – even the

The author doing his Frankenstein impression on an early rock tour with a New Zealand export, Sharon O'Neill.

women, who look more like Rogers than the men who look like Rogers.)

A friend told me about a nervous driver in Canterbury, who when he took his wife and two children out for a drive made them all wear motorcycle crash helmets inside the car. Once, they were stopped by a traffic officer, who took one look inside the car with the children's heads lolling about on their shoulders under the weight of the helmets and mum blinking at him through her visor — and waved them on out of an overwhelming sense of pity.

Orienteering is like watching Kenneth Branagh's *Hamlet*. You have to be pissed to sit through it and as a result you have only a hazy recollection at the end that Kenneth was onto a good idea. (I sat through it twice at the Embassy in Wellington with a bottle of bourbon and all I remember was that it was like orienteering.)

Orienteering is such an appalling name that you know that it had to have come from a university. A group of people follow a trail that someone else has left in the bush.

This very nearly caught on as something to do. But finally it didn't because, like men with veins sticking out on their legs, it is very unattractive. Like swimmers shaving their bodies to reduce drag in the water (ho, ho!) it is quite meaningless. But it does speak volumes about the human condition: of men and women straggling through the undergrowth of their experience, in the main, lost, but looking for clues.

Don't try and improve yourself. Just keep looking for clues.

This may be a difficult concept to grasp. It may be too difficult straight off to give up the liniment and the notion that the aerobics instructor actually fancies you. (He or she is gay, so forget it!)

Research has shown that if you think about exercise, little electrical impulses go out and tune up the muscles. How about that? There is a tiny gymnasium in your mind. Go to it.

If you have to, imagine that there is an instructor there who is a cheery, goofy guy called Chas. Enter the mind, enter the gymnasium, and get changed facing the locker. Hear the little locker click shut. Put your imaginary towel over your shoulder and go into the Big Room. Climb on board one of those machines that improves your ab-flabs.

Overlay your imaginary buttock clenching with another picture of how good you are going to look in Speedos next summer.

When you leave your gym of the mind, don't forget to give a big cheery wave to Chas. (Remember, he spends his whole life in your mind.)

You have now done all of the gym things. You are free to have fun. This is not as easy as it sounds. I spoke at a University Blues dinner a year or two back. There were synchronised swimmers (when someone proposed a toast, they raised their glasses in unison) and a lot of people got prizes because they played in a team which had beaten another team of underwater hockey players!

The worst thing about this whole evening was that these people were young and they didn't know that they were supposed to be fun. They had no idea. Somehow they survived the miracle of conception, birth, got a university education and still believed they were seriously important people.

We could dismiss these people out of hand, or say, "There goes another unfortunate experiment," but experience shows that they go on perpetuating their own delusions. They take over businesses, bureaucracies, politics and scare other people witless. So much so that no one says to them: "Did you seriously get a blue for underwater hockey?"

Speaking as a friend to the witless, I suggest you ask any self-opinionated, dark-suited CEO or interviewing officer what sort of interests he or she had at university. If the answer comes back, as it undoubtedly will, that, "I got a blue in hockey, swimming, rugby, etc etc," fall over backwards laughing. Grab the desk for support and turn it over. Get up on your feet and crash into the wall cabinet, putting your elbow through the glass. Loosen your tie and heave your lunch on the carpet. Finally saying, "I don't think you're the man (woman) for me," wipe your mouth on the curtain and leave.

Suzanne Paul and me at the Silly Grin finals.

If you don't leave that individual a changed person for life, I'd be very surprised. And you will be held in high regard by a grateful nation.

Then we come to the books which tell you how to get rich or improve your IQ. Getting rich is easy if you have money to start with or you are determined (like Suzanne Paul of Natural-Glo fame).

Suzanne is a delight. She knows exactly how to play Suzanne (she of the harsh voice and put-on sillies). She is living proof, following years of selling vibrating pillows in bleak shopping malls, that if you decide to be someone and you have the guts – that person you will become.

A lot of the literature seems to be about self-actualisation. I haven't had time to read it because I am actually very busy with my own opinions. However, if you insist on trying to improve yourself, brace yourself for the likely outcome: what if you are actually an arsehole?

A lot of people are. They don't mean to be. It's often genetic. So if you go down that road to self-discovery and at the far end you find yourself staring into a straining, puckered orifice, don't blame anyone else. You were the one who decided to confront yourself.

Bruce Morrison.

One of the directors of the *McCormick* programme, Bruce Morrison, himself no intellectual or philosophical slouch, made the comment over a crew dinner (the windup of a filming shoot) that I was afraid to confront myself. That I indulged in constant travel and activity to avoid facing myself on my own.

This is the kind of bear-pit baiting we do on filming expeditions in the absence of a real war. The objective is to find weak spots in the characters of your colleagues and drill in there until you hit pay dirt. The ultimate compliment you can give a fellow crew member is to urge them on, while he or she, scenting an opportunity over dinner or drinks at the end of a hard day's filming, is able to psychologically slit open a colleague from neck to waist, grab a handful of entrails, place a foot on their neck and pu . . . ll – until they come free in the hand.

Bruce Morrison was, as always, perfectly correct. As a television frontperson, I am a suppurating sore of denial.

But what's your problem?

If you find at the end of a process of self-examination that you are a fairly low order of human being (bottom-feeders, we call them in the crew) like a pro-gun lobbyist for

TWO SERIOUS PEOPLE!

"PULLING THEMSELVES TOGETHER"

Top Broadcaster
KIM HILL

GARY McCORMICK
1997 Entertainer of the Year

A SHOW FULL OF FUN, WIT AND POLITICS.

example, or someone who talks through the pictures, the consequences are then yours and yours alone.

In the case of the gun lobbyist, your hobby is tied up with destructive macho power and it is unlikely to change before a penis extension operation. If you talk in the pictures and I am in the same theatre, the consequences will be that I will, first, ask you to be quiet and, second, come right on over and ask you to leave.

Kim Hill and I went to see *Titanic* in Hastings while we were on a summer tour of (predominantly) vineyards. What a great tour it was! But on a rare afternoon off, we went to the two o'clocks (movies).

Unfortunately, an eighteen-year-old sheep herder from the southern Hawke's Bay decided to sit in the movie and make what he thought were very funny remarks at the top of his voice. Because we all grew up in a country where:

> a) large pimply faced drongos are regarded as "hard cases"; and
>
> b) we would sit and eat our own fingers rather than "cause a fuss"

he thought he was going to *be* the two o'clocks. He was his own matinee idol.

Because we are so polite, they take the All Black tests off free-to-air TV ("We should have seen it coming" – Jock Hobbs), let your ultimate bully, Rob Muldoon, run the country for eternity, introduce domestic departure taxes at local airports (no, I'm still not paying) and allow Maori activist Arthur Harawira to attack an actor at the launching of a book, *Paradise to Come* (!), and get "restorative justice" (a $475 fine to the victim, an educational course and asked to teach people Maori values and history!).

As a television frontperson and a suppurating

sore, etc etc, I am very dependent on other

people's fantasies

to fill in the gaps in my life.

Which is why the movies are so important to me. I became Kate Winslet for several weeks.

Which is why I had to ask the bozo to leave and twist his ear, using the lobe to help him to understand that I meant it.

When he left, we were able to sit back and watch the big ship go down, right to the point where Leo and Kate are lying around in the water.

I found it much more satisfying than watching Ralph (or is it Raeff) Fiennes declaring he would come back to the cave for the Englishwoman in *The English Patient*. (When she asked him if he would come back, he should have faked a coughing fit, rather than lie.)

Self-improvement is a cut above self-absorption but it's got nothing on self-satisfaction.
- Be a couch potato.
- Orientate yourself.
- Drink bourbon and, like Hamlet, dream of all the people you'd like to stab through the arras.

The TV

Micr

Crew as ocosm

CHAPTER 4

Ice TV presenter Jon Bridges has come out publicly in defence of wearing **sandals**. He wanted 1998 to be the Year of the Sandal!

Most people see sandals as an indication of some kind of mental disability, or as an affectation sported by computer nerds and pseudo-intellectuals — men with tufts of hair sprouting from their nostrils and ears. Yet Jon is none of these things.

Jon's people (the Generation X-ers) flocked to see the Jim Rose Circus. This is a somewhat unusual show where Sumo women wrestle and tattooed men lift weights with their private parts. The Paramount Theatre in Wellington was filled to capacity with men and women wearing sandals and plaid trousers.

To have elevated carelessness into a dress code is quite an achievement. Baggy trousers, sloppy shirts, squares, plaids . . . being cool and unaffected is important to Generation X. They wage war with anonymity by dressing like motel curtains.

They don't want to be famous and have a gentle disdain (as much as they can bring themselves to be interested) for people who show off. They do feel the need to mutilate themselves by way of tattoos and nipple rings (pain being an abrupt reminder of existence).

You don't have to understand what drives this generation to make itself unattractive but you do have to recognise the phenomenon – for reasons that I will explain later.

As a child of the sixties and excitable, I can't talk to them without feeling juvenile. I feel like I'm talking to someone's father.

Being in Australia at the time the One Nation party surged to prominence in the Queensland elections, it was interesting to see how quickly fear, insecurity and suspicion of (and I quote) "shiny-arsed politicians" can translate into political power.

One Nation believes that 8 per cent unemployment can be solved by halting immigration (no mention of any upskilling or training of the work force) and promises 2 per cent interest rates on loans and the printing of money to make up for any shortage. They are in la-la land.

The most disturbing aspects of the party are their racism and their deep antipathy towards anyone who thinks along different lines to their own deeply conservative outlook.

Judgments on humankind are better to come from the Land of Chortle. Where would we be without the diversity of human types which causes us so much admiration and amusement? Tuku Morgan's boxer shorts have become a metaphor for an era in New Zealand politics. I prefer to take the emphasis off the individual and say that New Zealand was a happier place when men wore Y-fronts, taking one pair away for a three-day footy trip and turning them back to front on the second day!

This may sound as if, from a writer's perspective, other people exist for the purposes of entertainment.

They do.

Life is a multiplex.

We have about us a battery of learned ideas. That icebergs contain six-sevenths of their bulk underwater (not true), that red wine should be opened to let it breathe (not true), that women button their blouses on the opposite side to distinguish them from men's shirts (not true – it came about as a result of servant girls having to dress their mistresses from the front?!!).

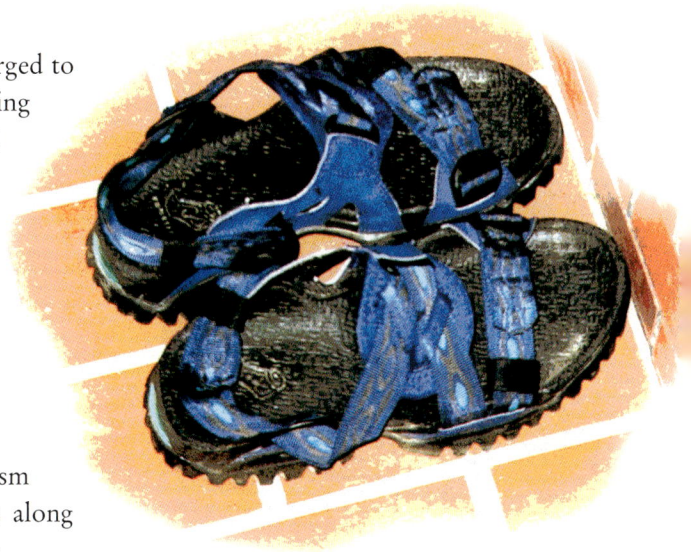

The McCormick crew's own Generation X-er, Simon Parsons, being observed carefully by Dunedin landlord (and part-time sound operator) John Patrick.

The importer of Timex watches has the nerve to tell us that the statement "water resistant to 30m" does not mean you can dive or swim with the watches. It means only that the watches have been tested in a pressure chamber to three bars of pressure. Follow that if you can!

The language is full of duplicity and carelessness. It is used by unscrupulous salespeople to further their commercial objectives.

The silly notions we grew up with, though, are very revealing and form the fabric against which we can measure other people's silly, but equally entertaining ideas.

The *McCormick* crew has a Generation X-er in its midst – a likeable cameraman called Simon Parsons. This cheery, hardworking lad has the dress sense of a feral creature. He wears hats with a picture of Bart Simpson on them! His catchphrase is Homer Simpson's "Duh!" One of his eyes – the one not attached to the viewfinder – looks away at a tangent. When he points the camera at me, the peculiar eye stares in a demented fashion off to the left. It makes him look like a pirate in plaid trousers.

There will be those who would argue that people in plaid trousers should be put on a remote island somewhere. But I know Simon Parsons (or Simon Parsonette, as we call him) and I will fight to keep him off the island for as long as I can.

I form part of the backdrop of Simon's life but I am careful not to ask him what impression he has of me. I'm sure I amuse him greatly and I suspect that, like many of his generation, he sees me as one of the "old guard" of television presenters – someone who maintains a certain crusty status and is fond of getting his own way. (Temperament in my case is merely frustration born out of the certainty that comes of being right.)

The truth is that Simon's generation must be treated with respect. In twenty or thirty years, they will be the ones administering the intravenous drips (although hopefully not Simon – with that eye!).

The explosion of cafe society in New Zealand reflects the fact that Generation X has now become the dominant culture.

Wooden floors and acid jazz ensure that hearing impaired (older) people cannot participate.

I suffer from "surfer's ear" – growth of the bone which covers the ear canal as a result of prolonged exposure to cold water. I can't hear anything in a cafe. (Being deaf has a certain number of advantages when you've reached my age and learned everything you need to know. It enables you to filter out monologues from self-improvers and people who tell you things for your own good.)

Strut and Fret . . .

I felt quite at ease (as people with disabilities who are in good hands do) when I went on an inspection tour of the future with Wellington actor Miranda Harcourt. Wellington has become the most interesting of our cities because it falls neatly into the introspection zone – anatomically located above the midriff (occupied by provincial centres like Palmerston North and Hamilton or Ashburton and Timaru in the south) and well above the erogenous zone, which is clearly Auckland.

It was Auckland, of course, which set the trend towards the "cafe as life experience". A 1970s "minimalist" Auckland restaurant called Five Columns had only three columns. One night I attended and found only one leaf of toilet paper in the loo!

In one Wellington cafe recently I finished reading two newspapers and, in the absence of a rubbish bin, stacked them neatly under the table. I told the young waitress about this.

"You put them on the floor!" she exclaimed in a manner which left no doubt that this was completely beyond the bounds of decent behaviour. She would have to pick it up, you see. The staff in the worst of these places are not workers. They do not even pretend to be actors between jobs. They are human ornaments whose decorative lives we are blessed with.

I would like to have burned the place down, as Jack Nicholson would have done. I didn't (which I now regret) and word spread so that, while I was touring with Miranda, a cafe owner near to the scene of the 1997 Newspaper Disaster shut the door of his cafe in our faces. This could have posed a serious threat to Miranda's health, who like good actors anywhere must have a constant flow of high-grade caffeine in her bloodstream. (She has an account at the Lido.)

I am not making the fashionable case for the return of the old inner-city public bar. I am still being confused by drinkers at the former Duke bar in Wellington, who are convinced that I drank there for years with the late Bruno Lawrence, James K. Baxter and Sam Hunt. I never set foot in the place. (Nowadays I have stopped arguing about it and can regale an audience with many anecdotes about the great days at the Duke!)

What do films and television have in common? Caffeine! (Here with Miranda Harcourt.)

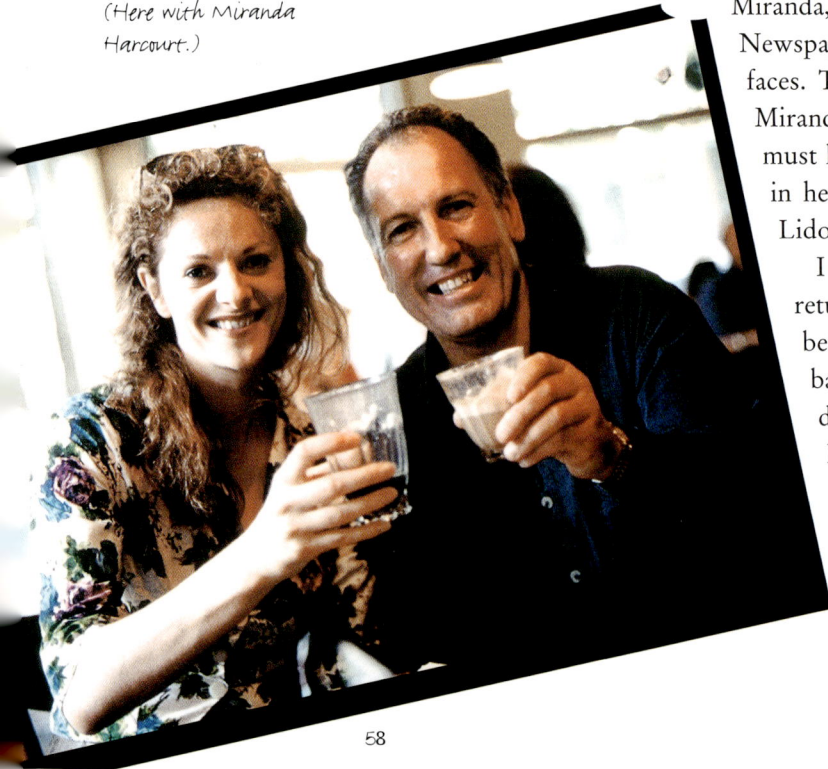

How do actors manage to remember who they are? Miranda (like her mother, Dame Kate) and Rima Te Wiata possess the actor's sensitivity and yes, a vulnerability, combined with a strength which seems to enable them to work through multiple roles, sometimes back to back and horrendous hours of work.

Rima had just finished work on *Via Satellite* when the *McCormick* crew arrived at the door of her Auckland address. She looked completely wrung out. I climbed into bed with her (in a pantomime kind of way) only to find as we leaned against the wall drinking tea that the bed began to slip away. We gently slid (neither of us acknowledging it) down the wall. A very funny sequence (which I don't think made its way into the programme), brilliantly played out.

The author and Sam Hunt during the colourful days when Sam lived opposite the popular Southern Cross Hotel in Wellington.

That is the kind of silliness which makes working in television worthwhile. It has been added to the fund of stories which make film crew reunions and dinners feasts of hilarious story-telling.

A male actor accosted Sam Hunt and me in a pub in Wellington (not the Duke!) regaling us with the story of his life and beseeching us to join the world of theatre.

His somewhat overly dramatic exhortations were dismissed by Sam with the words: "We don't have to act, mate. We're the real fucking thing!"

I have wanted to be an actor – indeed have been an actor, joining half the country's thespian set on location in Auckland for the filming of *Shrimp on the Barbie*, which is now I see in the video stores as *The Boyfriend From Hell*. I was a policeman in *Starlight Hotel*, filmed in lovely Oamaru, and had to punch the lead Australian actor in the stomach – for real (he insisted). I wrote a newspaper column about it, which upset him and he threatened to walk off the job.

The Glamour Twins

COMEDY WITH CLASS

BELINDA TODD

GARY McCORMICK

The Perfect Hosts

FOR YOUR CONFERENCE :: PRODUCT LAUNCH
AWARDS NIGHT

CONTACT: PHONE: (06) 868 9816 :: FAX: (06) 868 9836

Belinda Todd and the author, touting for the position of New Zealand's own Royal Family.

Clairvoyant Marlene Marshall predicted I would have a major part in a feature film in 1998. Two weeks after I spoke with her, I was called for an audition. I did it (rather well) and never heard from them again. They have made a big mistake in not casting me.

Since that near-miss I've thought about how hard actors work – twelve-, fourteen-hour days, six or seven days a week, and I've gone off the idea. Even if they revisited *The English Patient*, making the sequel, *English Patient II*, and asked me to go back and see if the Englishwoman was still lying, waiting in the cave (she'd be crackling by now) I'd probably turn them down.

Why? Because if you have an uncertain equilibrium (faulty gimbals, as director Bruce Morrison would say) and have to be too many other people, you might lose sight of the horizon!

(This is dealt with in another helpful chapter about how to handle your personal crises.)

Television is far less dangerous because it only involves marketing an extension of yourself. When I first worked for television, I was astonished how many of my colleagues regularly contacted magazines and newspapers to leak details of romances, health problems and public appearances.

Belinda Todd – a fountain of media energy, now with Communicado – taught me a lot about how to handle the media in professional terms. I met her during the Wellington celebrity street car race. Matthew Ridge, Bill Ralston, Sean Fitzpatrick and Kerre

Woodham, among others, were all involved in the race. Bill (in a noble gesture aimed at avoiding a collision with Ms Woodham) rammed head-first into a concrete block the size of Te Papa).

The race was a fascinating clash of cultures.

The sporting heroes, while very friendly socially, were determined to win at all costs. We so-called "media stars" were determined to look our absolute best while losing. During a practice lap in Taupo, I ran Matthew Ridge off the road and to this day cannot forget the look of pure fury on his face. (Mind you, that may have been because I borrowed his car in Sydney when he was playing for Manly and left Aussie with a huge parking fine which I think he had to pay.)

Belinda was very accomplished with the publicity machine. Whenever a photographer was in the vicinity, she would recline in her sporty overalls on the bonnet of one of the cars, helmet tucked beneath her arm. She appeared on the cover of everything.

Paul Holmes is another consummate media professional. The *McCormick* programme took Paul back to Haumoana, where he grew up, principally because of the number of celebrity debates in which Paul has told yarns about his golden upbringing in Hawke's Bay. Stories about bridges, cowsheds and the local fire brigade, delivered with twinkling, self-deprecating humour.

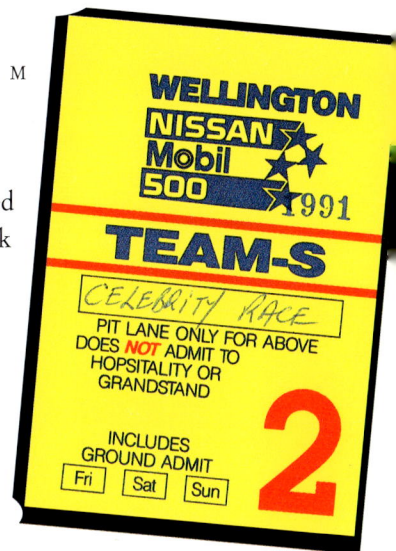

The tag that proves you once got into the pits!

Paul Holmes in Haumoana, about to embark on a black shirt phase.

Tom Scott — one of the funniest and most determined people I know. Forearms as big as the average human thigh.

There is a boyish sense of mischief about Paul which comes through from time to time (and more so lately) in his television work. There is also a single-minded toughness, almost a ruthlessness, which comes into play as quickly as you can change channels.

He is the Crown Prince of New Zealand television. Both the Prime Minister and Leader of the Opposition attended his well-publicised marriage – for which there has since been a media price to be paid.

The very day the breakup of his marriage to Hine and involvement with Fleur Revell hit the papers, Paul had a speaking engagement in New Plymouth. It was a debate with Ginette McDonald, Tom Scott, Raybon Kan and me at the Opera House.

Paul had to front up to some fierce ribbing, which included Ginette McDonald's widely reported jest that had she known about Paul's interest in younger women she would have been happy for Paul to treat her as two 23-year-olds! He handled it extraordinarily well in front of a capacity house of Taranaki folk, many of whom you might have expected to be less than sympathetic.

In the middle of the year, he wrote some newspaper columns for the *Herald* which were personal and revealing. They highlighted the difficulty faced by a public figure who has gone through a difficult time, particularly one whose job requires him to be opinionated and, at times, abrasive. It is a lonely (and yes, yes – well-paid) job.

Does anyone want to be famous that much? There is no shortage of people wanting the job. But they want it before they have any idea of what it means in personal terms.

A film crew is very much like a rock 'n' roll band. There's the lead singer (me), guitarist (cameraman or camerawoman), bass guitar (sound operator) with the director and production assistant alternating on the drums (setting the rhythm).

Yvette Thomas is the band's manager. Yvette literally gave her right arm while filming the *Heartland* programme on Lawrence. (It was very badly broken when a barge we were filming hit a riverbank at speed. We were braced for an accident but did not take into account an iron bar attached to the vehicle ramp which came down and smashed her to the deck.) Sometimes Yvette has to make the type of decisions about work and conditions which could result in Ginger Spice leaving the band!

Our executive producer (a kind of record company executive who holds the power of life and death over our collective future) is William Grieve. He is so high up the corporate ladder that you can only see him on a clear day. His head is often swathed in clouds. (Bruce Morrison is a director and executive producer, but we see more of him because Bruce travels with the crew more often.) William is assisted in mounting numerous projects by accountant Felicity Letcher. (Felicity's cheery voice on the phone defuses many a potential problem.)

While on location, I spend many hours in the truck while the crew attend to filming detail. This time is spent productively, either scribbling notes on bits of paper for my weekly talks with National Radio's Kim Hill or creating mischief.

Yvette Thomas, producer: Her beguiling smile masks an iron will.

Being mischievous is a very serious calling.

Truman Capote used to wear three sets of glasses: clear lenses when he was telling the truth (which wasn't often), darker lenses (but you could still see his eyes) when he wanted to fib, and impenetrable dark lenses when he wanted to lie outright about other people. The "three shades of the truth" as his (few) friends would say.

As a mature adult I appreciate the fabric of silly and mischievous ideas which, if laid wall to wall, helps to refurbish the mind. It is a selfishly enjoyable pastime but it gives a great deal of pleasure to embellish real events so that they become an entertainment.

I once managed to come across William Grieve with his arm down the front of an elderly gentleman's trousers. I discovered him in this compromising position behind a barn out in Ranfurly. (William was trying to assist the man who, having suffered a stroke, found himself unable to adjust his winter longjohns at a critical time.) I have told this story to anyone who will listen and have recommended that posters with photos of William on them be placed around old folks homes to alert the elderly ("If you see this man loitering . . . ")

Bruce Morrison, whose CV includes work with the BBC, and directing such films as *Constance, Shaker Run*, my very own *Bay Boys*, and *The Road To Jerusalem*, is blessed with a mop of thick, curly hair. I mention this in passing because during the studio filming of *McCormick Country*, an idiosyncratic Kiwi talk show much appreciated with hindsight, I was able to spread rumours that his hair is permed. This may seem like a petty exercise but it causes enormous enjoyment for me — particularly when I hear Bruce denying it to total strangers.

I even went to the trouble to "apple-pie" his bed in a motel in Wellington this year. Bruce always works late and I knew that when he finally crawled into bed at 2 or 3 a.m.

his brain would be so tired he would not be able to work out why he couldn't push his feet down to the bottom of the bed and would probably sleep with his chin on his knees.

The **unspeakable cruelty** of picking on the chronically fatigued is what makes a juvenile, pathetic, **mindless prank** so enjoyable. I learned about this kind of thing in Billy Bunter books.

I am telling you about what many will see as childish forms of behaviour because it helps to show how cheerful, destructive people like me, with a low boredom threshold, can be.

Bruce is a pensive kind of individual not given to vulgar outbursts of extroverted behaviour like my own and highly regarded in the industry for his directorial powers. He comes from the School of Quiet Direction where a nod is as good as a wink. Like certain skilful photographers, he can be both there and not there at the same time.

The crew (from left): Swami Hansa, Setu ("Second Biggest Island in the Fijian Group") Lio, Simon Parsons, the author, Yvette Thomas, director Bruce Morrison. On the ground (humbling himself): sound operator John Patrick.

The band has a roadie – part-time European professional rugby league player Setu Lio (nicknamed the "Second Biggest Island in the Fijian Group" by director Sean Duffy). Setu, when not working for us, goes, we believe, to Spain or somewhere and plays league. (We promise to deny this if tortured by Spanish tax authorities.)

Setu, apart from being the Second Biggest Island in the Fijian Group Whose Primary Export Is Sugar Cane, does most of the inter-location driving of the Gazza-mobile. He can drive all night and still smile in the morning. In fact, we have been bloody lucky to keep him!

The lead guitarist, by virtue of age and experience, while still terminally young, is Swami Hansa. Swami is a noted cameraman whose name was adopted because of his religious beliefs. He has had an interesting life, having done "porridge" somewhere in one of those countries where they put you in jail first and ask questions later. Cool under pressure, he has filmed in helicopters while they fell from the sky and crashed. Normally I would worry about the ambitions of a lead guitarist – most of whom would rather be the lead singer – but Swami is not afflicted with earthly ambitions of that kind. I have always been in awe of him.

Aussie Clint Bruce is the perfect cameraman-cum-guitarist – the Ron Wood of our group. He is the only person to walk into the deep end of a swimming pool – while filming me talking to advertising guru Len Potts. A splash and he was gone (along with $130,000 worth of camera).

The directors – Bruce, Sean Duffy, Jonathon Cullinane – quite often say out loud that they are present to serve me, and to make me look good.

I sometimes detect a note of sarcasm, or self-serving ingratiation in their remarks, but so long as I remain aware of possible coup attempts there is no reason why I should not remain The Presenter ("the meat", "the talent") for some time to come.

I see that certain MPs have raised in Parliament questions about how much certain television presenters are paid, stating a belief that no job in television can be worth "that much".

They are probably right to say it. Except that work in televison has about as much permanence as soap in the shower (like their own jobs) and under the free market regime, hay must be made while the watery sunlight continues to shine.

The bass player in this veteran band is John Patrick from Dunedin. When he disappears from our midst to pursue natural history work, recording the mating of the kakapo, or wetas performing around tiny maypoles, his role is taken by the genial and jovial Eugene Arts. But in the main, throughout the *Heartland* years until the present day, John has been the principal sound recordist of the group.

John has all the character traits of the solid and decent South. Frugal and wise, it seems to us that he often ends the week with more per diems (daily allowances) than he began with. John's forte is punning (if you regard punning as being of any value to the human race – which we don't) so we have to lower him to the ground and hit him from time to time.

I used to believe that sound operators went slowly mad as part of the normal course of events.

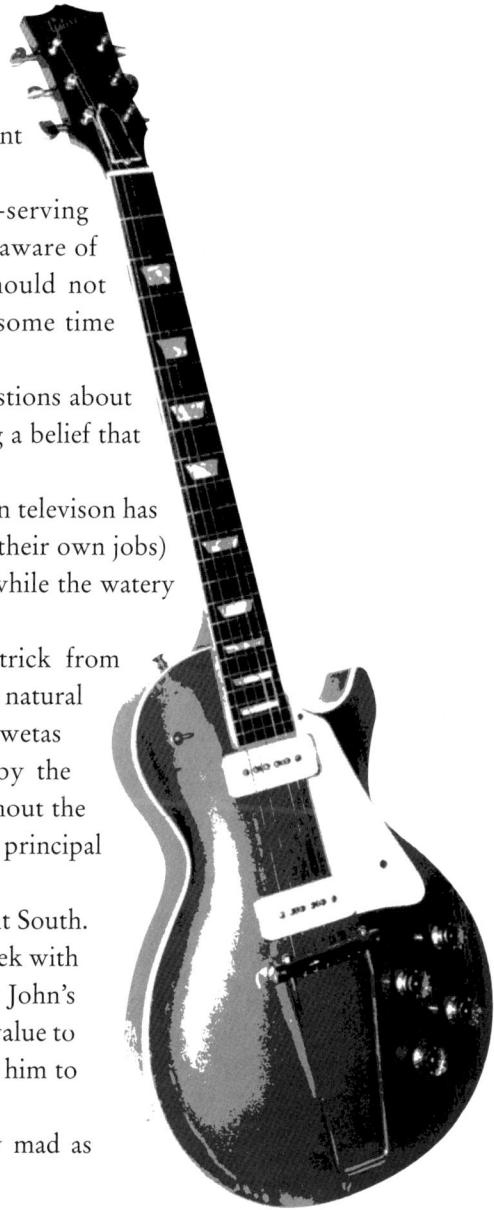

They hear things that we mere mortals cannot hear and eventually declare that God has started talking to them.

Then they realise that if God was going to talk to anyone, it is highly unlikely that he would bother with a sound operator. (They then go very quiet and have to be replaced.)

This has not yet happened to John. Perhaps because he pretends to be only a sound operator. It has come to the attention of the rest of the crew that he buys tenement buildings, which he then lets to students, fifteen or sixteen to a room. He owns a holiday home in Wanaka and is known to be richer than the Suhartos.

I am trying to encourage everyone not to like him, but this is proving difficult.

The sound operator is attached to the cameraman by a wire and the two are seldom separated. It remains to be seen if, on the sorry day that John or Swami leaves this mortal coil, the cord can be severed quickly enough to save the other.

People do ask me how we find the people we interview on the programme. Names come to me and to the Morrison Grieve office, where they are researched by Bernadine Lim, Kirsten Matthew, Jeremy Cvitanovich and Roy Colbert. Mike Kavanagh – now back in London doing some fabulously interesting work for the BBC – produced the first series and kept a wary eye out for information from the field which could lead to expensive mistakes. We have to check about a bit as it is not uncommon for interest groups (some appointed by the nominee themselves!) to forward names and declare what interesting people they are. As a rule in the televison game, as in life, the people who declare themselves interesting are not.

Which brings us to Sean Duffy. Sean was the director of the *Heartland* great: "Wainuiomata: Beyond Nappy Valley", which nearly had me lynched. I was burned in effigy in the shopping mall. Sean also directs *McCormick*.

He is not without talent as an actor, having been a policeman in both *Mortimer's Patch* and *Plainclothes* to mention just two of his many roles. So good, in fact, that he was beaten up in the toilets of the old Gluepot Hotel in Auckland by a criminal who thought he was an undercover cop!

As mentioned in a previous chapter, Sean has offered to be my friend and I think he is sincere about this. But there can be no doubt that of the rivalries tearing at the fabric of the band as an entity, the Duffy-McCormick one would have to be the most serious.

On the road, summer of '97-'98, with Kim Hill and bluesman Hammond Gamble.

Sean maintains that he has no desire to be a television star. You could take that at face value if you didn't know that he lived in Mt Albert and his idea of recreation is to take his darling son Reilly on a track-suited excursion to the St Luke's shopping mall.

There is nothing wrong with the mall as malls go. It is like any other, with jangling music, the scraping of supermarket trolleys, screams of small children, etc etc. But even Reilly has begun to ask plaintively, "Do we have to go to the mall again, Daddy?" Sean is content to sit there, watching life go clanking by.

Or is he? I happen to know that there are more dramatic roles ahead for Sean, some being written especially for him. There are people who want to get him out of Mt Albert.

My deepest fear is that they will unearth the real, the human, Duffy. There is a lot of compassion in the man, the result of sitting in the mall for hours on end. He quite frequently rebukes me on location with the words, "You just don't care!"

(I try to explain that, because my life is so full, the space left for the kind of beery, blinking, mawkish, who-will-look-after-the-little-kittens sentimentality is very small.)

One of my ambitions is to do a television series with Sean in which I take him to see the sea for the first time.

At the end of the day, a television programme is the sum of all its performing and well-edited parts. Ken (Sir Kenneth) Sparks, Tim Woodhouse and Dermot McNeillage spend days in a dark room doing the editing. They appear to enjoy it (or perhaps it is just the pleasure of seeing the light when we let them out?). Nonetheless they do produce that increasingly elusive thing: the Kiwi TV programme – that most powerful of mediums which enables us to look at ourselves.

The medium that has taught me about working with people.

Different people.

Amusing people.

People who collect salt and pepper shakers.

Not ever (hopefully) One Nation people.

ADVANCE AUSTRALIA FAIR (THE POEM)

by Gary McCormick

(Written in response to the call for a poem as a preamble
to an Australian constitution.)

Advance Australia Fair, into the clear blue air
of a brand new day.
Where Woollan – gongs and Didgerees – do
and others try the best they can too.
Though Shane may be Warne, Ayer's a-rocking,
we haven't heard much of odometer clocking.
Advance Australia fairest!

Where jackaroos do and jackaroos don't
we're coming to Auckland with a much stronger boat.
You can bet your sweet life that this one will *float*.
Advance Australia – with inflatables.

So it's raise your head high and shoulders back.
If your neck is hurting – adjust the strap.
It's a mighty fine country, going all the way back –
so keep your hands on the steering wheel, Maureen.

There is so much in verse an Aussie can handle
about beaches and barbies and uranium landfill,
so this will be only a modest preamble –
while we look for a word which rhymes with constitution.

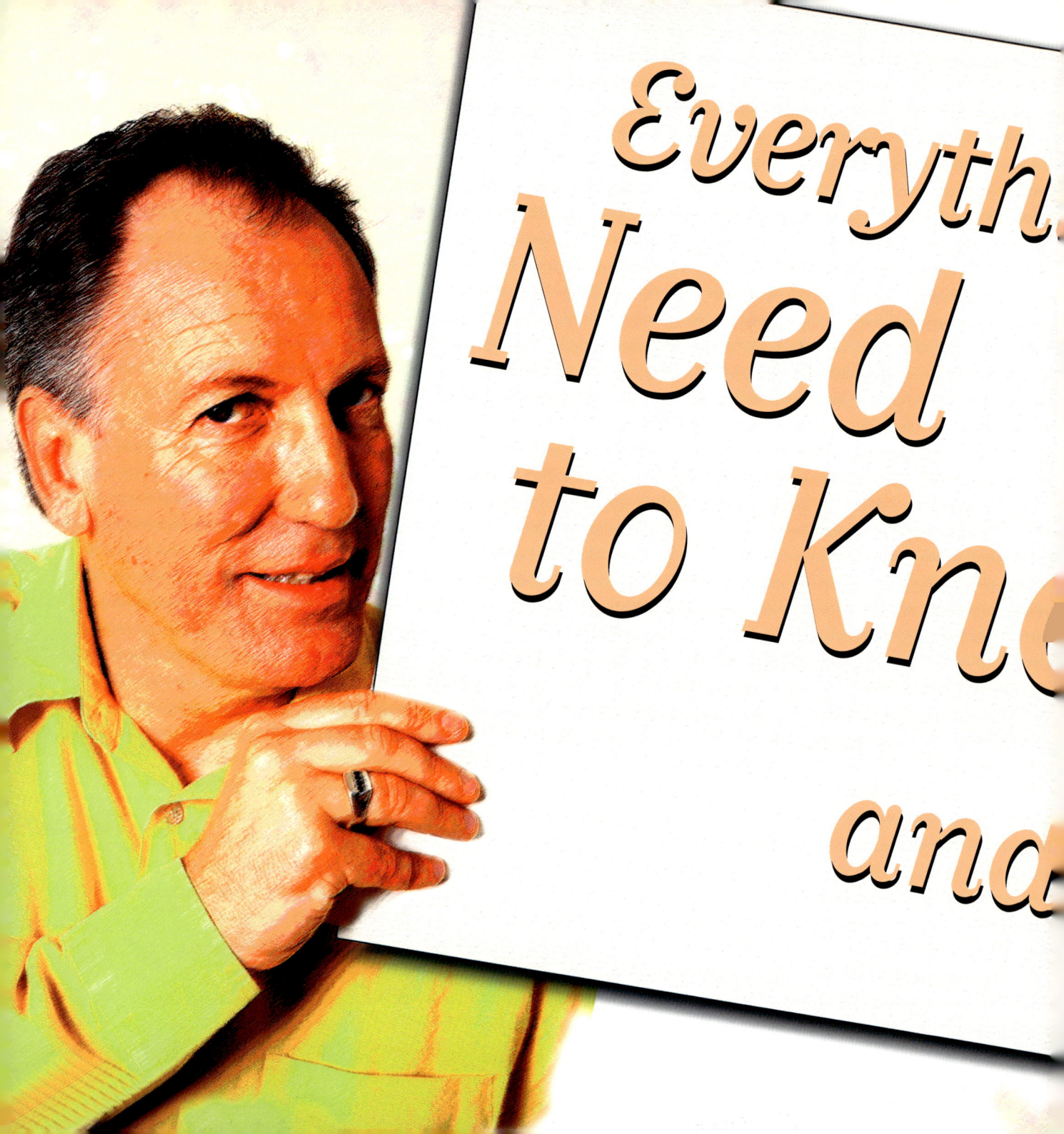

Everyth...

Need

to Kn...

and

ng *You Will Ever*

W About Men

Women

CHAPTER **5**

In June 1998, I attended the large agricultural expo at Mystery Creek. My job was, as always, to keep up the spirits of farmers who were **drowning hay bales of cash** because of the drop in the value of the New Zealand dollar.

There are none so bold and none so true, as those who dance the how-do-yer-do . . .

– words of a European folk song (circa AD 1210) found tucked inside a Portuguese helmet found on Ninety Mile Beach.

Not all farmers benefited from this change in the dollar's value, but it is hard at large gatherings to tell the drought-stricken farmers from the wallet-stricken ones. As a rule, neither party goes around throwing their hats in the air because they know that the dollar can go ballistic at any moment and lock on to the space station *Mir* for several years.

The only way you can tell a temporarily rich farmer from a poor one is the number of sandwiches the rich ones get offered at the bank hospitality tent. Some of the more confident will splash out and purchase two lengths of plastic piping to hit cows with.

I asked if there were any problems in the rural hinterland that I could help with. A woman in a beautifully hand-knitted jersey said she was worried about the number of hedgehogs who walk onto the road and get run over. (A friend of mine used to call them "hedgepigs" – isn't that lovely?)

Only a woman would raise an issue like that. Women are very protective of small things – even if they have spikes. It is surprising that women haven't mounted a campaign to save metal trouser zips. (By way of contrast, the only concern raised by a man was what could be done to stop erosion along the Mt Maunganui foreshore. I explained that the sand was moving because it couldn't afford to stay there.)

I don't know anything about hedgehogs because something stopped me learning about them many years ago.

I am lucky enough to have a stop/go switch in my brain. Sean Duffy, the distinguished television director from Mt Albert, would describe it as a neon sign on the door of a room, flashing the words "Don't Come In Here". My brain has always stopped short of the door with the word "Hedgehog" written on it. A woman, on the other hand, would go in, throw back the curtains and open the windows to let it air.

The lovely thing about women is that it's absolutely no problem for them to feel love for a hedgehog. It requires no special effort. The brain and the heart make an immediate connection and simply short out with a buzzing sound and sparks like those electrical transformers by the sea on a stormy night.

As it happened, I was able to relate to the questioner at Mystery Creek a true story about a woman driver who swerved ("What if you follow someone with unswerving devotion – and they swerve?") to avoid a hedgehog and rolled her car.

The lucky hedgehog could still be seen making its slow way across the road as the tearful driver was explaining to the police what had happened. Along came a male driver who stopped to see if he could help at the accident site. He ran over the hedgehog.

It was pointed out to him that he had squashed the central reason for the accident.

"Oh no!" he said, "that's the third one I've run over this morning!"

Men are not insensitive. It's just that they don't have time to be sensitive. Sensitivity is something men put off until they've got time to concentrate on it. They don't have the hedgehog response mechanism built into them.

We die younger than women because of this repressed sensitivity. Death comes to us just as we feel a huge emotional breakthrough is around the corner! Research shows that the last thing most men feel before dying is that something big is about to happen.

Men grieve for something throughout their lifetimes. We have an unspoken sense of loss. Some people believe it is the piece of skin we lost at the time of circumcision. In the absence of any other explanation, this will do.

Think about the giant squid. It lives in Cook Strait so far down that it is dark all of the time. Squid do not have great eyesight, which is why the Japanese manage to catch them by shining light on the water. Squid, with their sad little eyes, think that someone has finally designed a television picture powerful enough to be seen by squid.

The giant squid stays down the bottom, as lonely as can be. It can't even see girl squid!

So it fires off five-centimetre sperm projectiles every now and then hoping one of them will connect. (A squid family reunion is full of surprises!)

Isn't there some kind of analogy here for the Kiwi male?

Before we get off the subject of squid and to give you the opportunity to decide if you like the analogy or not, take a look at MALE HEALTH.

You would be silly not to because it is going to be THE NEXT BIG THING. You will need to be able to talk about it on panel discussions and in cafes because a very interesting gap in conversation is opening up.

For the past twenty years, women's health ("the unfortunate experiment") has been at the forefront of public concern. But even the women most committed to women's issues are becoming aware that you've got to give the other side a go. If you don't, you start to look like the Canterbury rugby team beating the West Coast 123 nil.

Women are starting to sit back

and wait for men to talk about their testicles.

You will notice that even the names given to men's parts are designed to make them sound ridiculous: "testicles", "penis", "scrotum". "Breast" and "vagina" sound like boxes of chocolates in comparison. This is a large part of the reason why men find it difficult to talk about their health.

The men most likely to suffer testicular cancer are slim, smoke and wear tight underpants.

"Hey, I'm slim and . . . er . . . my pants are tight . . . do you know what I mean?"

Men have a lot of heart attacks. Their artery walls thicken as a form of self-defence. However, relief is at hand. The answer to arteriosclerosis lies in eating some of the stuff you find in the bottom of budgie cages. You guessed it – chitosan – a substance extracted from squid skeletons!!

If you have ever doubted that there is an overall plan, a grand symmetry to life, the existence of chitosan must prove it. To think that the lonely old squid comes through at the end and turns out to be a softener for the human heart is almost beyond belief!

Men have been under sustained attack since the first Portuguese sailor left his helmet behind on Ninety Mile Beach. Roles have changed. The man is no longer the provider. He cannot have children.

He thinks a hedgehog is a tiny judder bar. Being male is no longer sexy.

In late 1994, Health Waikato lodged a complaint with the Advertising Standards Complaints Board about an advertisement in which a forestry worker played the first few notes of a Waikato Draught theme song on his chainsaw. Health Waikato claimed that the movement of the chainsaw at hip height was both sexually suggestive and aggressive. (It used to be called "air guitar".)

Regardless of the outcome of the complaint, it would seem that chainsaws are no longer the aphrodisiac they once were. Yet crime statistics show that one of the most frequently stolen items in New Zealand today is the chainsaw.

It's time we men caught up.

Women over the past year have been winning hunting and shooting competitions over men. Men used to have a monopoly in killing defenceless creatures. Women have even started brawling at women's rugby matches.

Razor companies tell us that there are as many hairs on a woman's leg as there are on a man's chin, only they are in a different place.

Women believe that a sharp blade is more likely to cut them than a blunt blade and consequently use blades ten times longer ("furry logic").

Men have growing rates of depression and a growing number are swapping wallets for handbags with a little strap around the wrist.

A recent survey asked men:
● If they had ever used rhino horn?
● Did it make them paw the earth and charge headlong at potential partners?
● Had they ever faked sincerity in bed with their partners?

(NB. It turns out that rhino horn is actually made from the horn of a rhinoceros but there is no tiger in Tiger Balm. Kiwi men on deer velvet do tend to stand at the bar like the famous "Stag at Bay" paintings of the fifties. When you are in your fifties, you adopt the "Sag at Belt" look.)

(NB II. The hippopotamus is the biggest killer of humans on the African continent. It is not the hedgehog.)

The results indicate that a lot of men have been duped into using fake rhino horn so that while few remember what they did the previous night they can recall some great yarns about rugby trips some ten or fifteen years earlier.

The most damaging admission is (or will be when we publish the names and addresses) that 82 per cent of men have faked a measure of sincerity in bed. But as they claimed to have answered the questions honestly, we can't be too sure about the results.

Prominent Hamilton radio broadcaster Jacqui Fraser says that the difference between men and women is that men leave:

● empty plates in the fridge
● empty milk cartons in the fridge
● the cardboard centre of the toilet roll on the holder when the paper has run out.

Women can't make machinegun noises.

SO HOW CAN WE POSSIBLY GET TOGETHER?

Waiting for the smoke to clear.

It is impossible to overestimate the importance of subtlety in trying to woo a woman. In the fifties, a man needed Brylcreem and the ability to tie his shoelaces without assistance to get a wife.

In the sixties, both parties smoked a lot of dope and didn't know who they had married until the late seventies.

In the seventies, people stopped marrying until the smoke had cleared.

In the eighties, people married cautiously and with due diligence carried out on one another's assets and future earning power.

In the nineties, the situation is confused to the point where I can only trail out with a series of dots................

There may be no obvious solution but the following observations may help.

Most women know their hairdressers better than they know their partners. This is a matter of choice. A hairdresser is a non-threatening person who has little to say of any real depth and is able to blow through the social landscape like a fur-ball.

A world-wide manufacturer of toiletries recently announced that the Kiwi male's reputation for being more interested in grooming his car than himself is being challenged. Men now spend on average 23 minutes a day grooming themselves, sometimes stretching to 31 minutes for a special occasion (a motor show?).

There is nothing wrong with being clean.

For the right reasons.

It is not in anyone's interest to encourage vanity.

There is no harm in spitting on a comb for a wedding or funeral and applying the normal soap and water to the body parts which gather dust. If you can borrow a bit of the chardonnay and whip it under the armpits when no one is looking – fair enough!

But don't make hygiene an obsession.

You may have seen a lot of pictures around of a bloke called Calvin Klein. I have no idea who he is (in fact he appears to be several different people). But he is always looking down on you and he has cheekbones which stand out on his face as if they have nowhere to go.

If you are anything like me, you will be worried that Calvin is stalking you. You don't know why he is following you, or even what he does (apart from cheekbone exercises). But he does have an uncanny presence – like a shopping list on a fridge door. You feel there ought to be a point to him, but there isn't.

Many men suffer from performance anxiety, which is ironic because it's non-performance anxiety. Which is to say that the media wish-list of how a man shall behave is beyond the scope of most men.

Internationally, sperm counts are on the way down (perhaps the people counting them are getting tired) and men have been warned to stay away from tight underwear, industrial chemicals and caffeine.

You can avoid tight underwear by slimming but it is difficult to get away from industrial pollution – unless you wear your Y-fronts over your head and breathe slowly.

The problem of premature ejaculation has had more publicity than is helpful. It fails to arise out of a sense of anxiety. Whose fault is that? The Japanese economy was officially declared to be "in recession" in June 1998. The drought continues on the East Coast. Auckland loses the Super 12 cup. The All Blacks are running around like mad chooks and losing. Is that the fault of the poor sap between the sheets?!!

According to the natural human body clock, men are likely to be most sexually active around 7 a.m., which is precisely the time Mike Hosking and Susan Wood appear on breakfast television. Could they perhaps be mindful of this, stay off the Nikkei Index and get into something more revealing? Would it not be helpful to mention only those share prices going up and forget those on the way down?

Nature has ordained that lovemaking for men is the equivalent of an outdoor winter sport. The act of seduction and foreplay is like climbing a mountain. Sadly, by the time

Being in love with your car means you can change gear without having to shower first.

– old V8 proverb.

a woman is approaching the summit, suitably attired and with oxygen for emergencies, the man is back at base camp feeding the huskies.

Pressure and criticism of this perfectly natural (nature-ordained) behaviour does not help. The huskies will starve for starters.

For men, sex interrupts anxiety.

Television is partly to blame. The BBC paid an English couple £30,000 to allow themselves to be filmed having sex from the inside out. Why so much money? Presumably because of all the extras involved.

Manufacturers in Europe are currently testing a contraceptive system involving a hormone-testing device which will flash a green light when it is safe to have sex (there are no hedgehogs on the road) and a red light when there is a risk of pregnancy. No word on the orange light but it might pay to slow down.

Shere Hite (an actual person who likes to gossip) reveals that 84 per cent of American women are unhappy in their marriages, leaving 12 per cent who are having a fantastic time and 4 per cent who don't know. Ninety-eight per cent of women want more "verbal closeness" in their marriages.

(In a year's time, 98 per cent of American women will report an allergy to spittle in their ears.)

Chat magazine in the UK reports that 60 per cent of English women have fantasised about having sex with a doctor or a celebrity. Twenty-one per cent have never had an orgasm. Thirty-six per cent have said they have faked it to please their partner. Which raises the following questions:

- Does being fantasised about affect a doctor's performance?
- Who is this celebrity? (He can be taken off television.)
- How can you be sure you have never had an orgasm if you don't know what it's like?
- What's going to happen if men start faking how gratified they are at their partner's orgasms? (Flowers, tears, "I'd like to thank the director for having faith in me, etc etc.")

Among baboons, the higher the male ranks in the social hierarchy, the more sex he has. On a debating tour in July '98, Tom Scott told me that among herds of caribou, only a few dominant males get to shag the young females. The rest of the males have to stand to one side and wait for the stick men to die from exhaustion.

I see no reason to tell you this other than to highlight Scott's unusual interest in the sex life of the caribou.

LET'S TRY STAYING IN TOUCH!

Up to the age of 35 days, all embryo are women. After that, the SRY gene kicks in and gives women pink fingernails and mirrors on the backs of car sun-visors. Men get fingernails to store axle grease under.

Women's brains expand.

Men's brains say to themselves – this is a busy-enough place already – and shrink by 20 per cent.

We were once the same tiny creature. We must work together again to prevent the next phase of human development, which will be to take humanity out of human hands. We already have the anti-fat pill, Regaine, Viagra and a synthetic pheromone made out of human armpit sweat which drives women crazy.

It is going to be difficult to do anything spontaneously because you have to take the pill an hour before. (No one has explained what happens if you take the pill and she gets a headache.)

One day we are going to look back while we are crazily bonking one another's svelte bodies and say, "God, I'd give anything not to be a love machine!"

Or, "I wish I wasn't such a high-ranking baboon."

Sport

Their Games

Know

CHAPTER 6

— "By Ye shall Them"

People play games when there is nothing else to do. This is why we are so lucky to live in a country where most of the hedges are already trimmed, the pine trees stand neatly in rows and the lawns are cut of a Saturday morning.

These are the real games we are talking about. The completely futile ones. The pointless activities which reveal us for what we are – kids. Not the activities which the pretend grown-ups have hijacked for corporate "team-building" or the desperate prancing of the gym romancers.

Once the washing is out, there is not a lot else to do other than think about life, or what comes after it – death. The intellectual, and therefore more fragile, elite have professional spiritual advisers or counsellors to do the worrying for them. They are then able to join the rank and file splashing about in the mud. Sport is a great leveller.

Some might argue that sport has become too

organised, too professional and that the race these days is to the various jars of money available to the above-average player.

If you are lucky enough to be David Tua fighting an American by the name of Coffee, you can earn a sizable amount of money by keeping your eye on a flabby, hopelessly-out-of-condition American and tapping him once on the side of the face so that he falls down in seconds. Some people say that this kind of thing brings pro boxing into disrepute. Not so. It is merely an extension of the efficiency drives aimed at turning a profit in the shortest possible time.

Furthermore, promoters had the wit and wisdom to combine boxing with track and field. High-jumping boxing-style, as demonstrated by Tua's opponent on this occasion, involved standing still for a moment and then toppling forward. It's an event for the whole family and the Hillary Commission should do more to encourage it.

A nation in search of its soul. One of the key issues arising at Pull Yourself Together Party conferences is, "What are we going to do about the cricket?"

Ever since a few of the boys admitted smoking marijuana in a dressing room and some visiting players were accused of smoking Moroccan cigarettes, it has become obvious to the most drunken yobbo on the terraces that the nation is caught in some deep sporting malaise. Do our professional sports people think they are wankers?

Looking at the game of cricket in the broad light of day you would have to say that it doesn't have a lot going for it. Most of the spectators go along to steal elderly gentlemen's ties and make vulgar suggestions to passing young women. That is because very little happens on the field of play. Many of the players themselves would like the

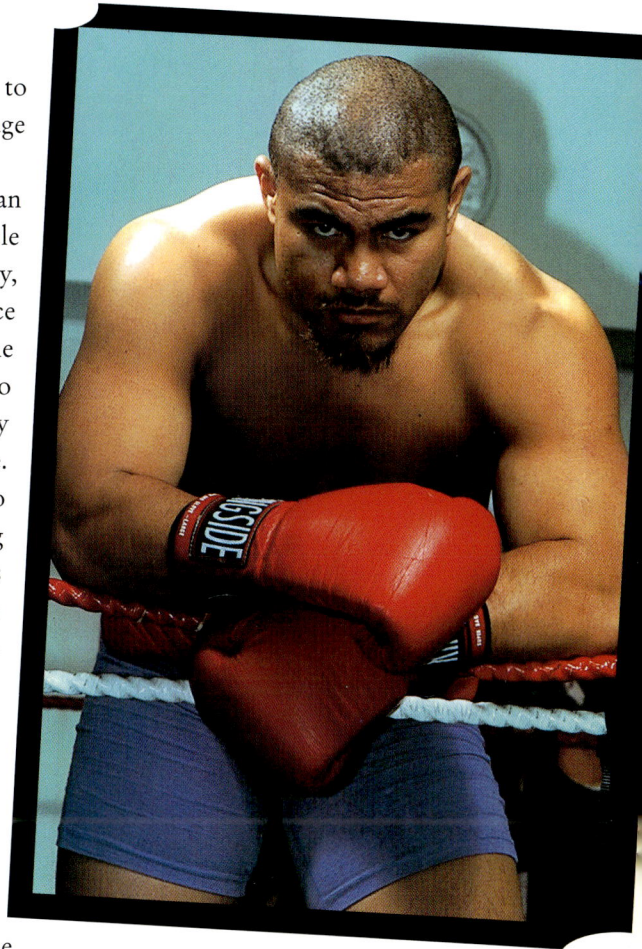

David Tua – will find an opponent worthy of him any day now!

PULL YOURSELF TOGETHER PARTY
POLICY FACT SHEET NO. 1

A draft document discussion paper on possible future options for a draft blueprint of the future.

- WOMEN TO BE ALLOWED TO CONTINUE TO HAVE THE BABIES IN NEW ZEALAND.

- SUBSIDY FOR INTERNAL LIGHTING OF WOMEN'S HANDBAGS.

- KIWI MEN TO BE ALLOWED TO CONTINUE TO SHOW OFF AROUND SWIMMING POOLS.

- SURF LIFESAVERS' "TIGHT-FITTERS" TO BE OBLIGATORY ON NEW ZEALAND BEACHES. (Research promised into combating "wedgies".)

- AFTERNOON SIESTA TO BE INTRODUCED (but not for schoolteachers!).

- BEEHIVE TO BE SHIFTED TO LEFT OF SOAMES ISLAND, WELLINGTON HARBOUR. (Once inhabitants smoked out.)

- SMALL GROUP TO RUN COUNTRY.

- ODOMETER WIND-BACKS TO BE PERMITTED ON OLD HOLDENS.

- SUPERANNUATION CANCELLED IN FAVOUR OF GENEROUS BART SIMPSON T-SHIRT HANDOUT.

- **BIRTH CONTROL.** Yes! No more giving birth wherever the aromatherapy instructor decides.

- **AUTOMATIC TELLER MACHINES** to be reprogrammed with better manners.

- **WOMEN'S AFFAIRS TO BE SEPARATED OFF IN A DIFFERENT COMPANY, RUN BY PROMINENT BROADCASTER KIM HILL, AND BASED IN THE COOK ISLANDS** (with corresponding tax advantages).

- **WAITANGI SETTLEMENTS.** Generous tracts of Australia to be given to anyone diddled in a hire purchase agreement.

- **THE ENVIRONMENT** (yawn!) to be retrenched. The trench to be lined by greenies, trampers, mountain bikers and other "saddles" who can't see the wood for the trees.

- **Y-FRONT ENQUIRY. (Y-not?)**

- **MARIJUANA NOT LEGALISED UNTIL THEY WIPE THE STUPID GRINS OFF THEIR FACES!**

- **LOCAL COMMITTEES TO DECIDE WEATHER TEMPERATURE ON TV.**

- **ARTS COUNCIL GRANTS:** Remove "feather-bedding" and over-manning in symphony orchestras and ballet companies. Money given only to painters who paint places we recognise. Generous subsidies for women with powerful thighs who play the cello.

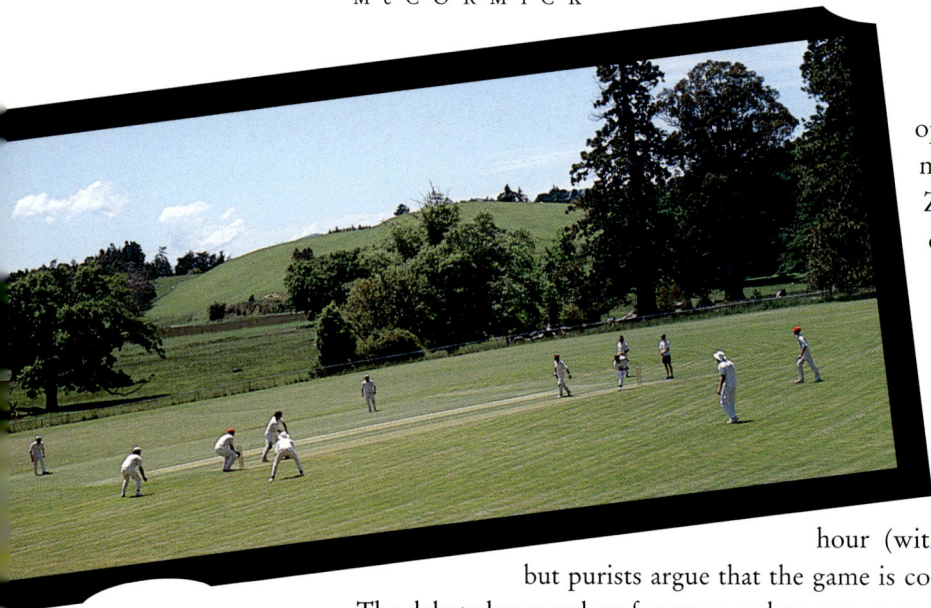

Cricket: A game which gives the absence of life, meaning.

opportunity to read a book or a magazine. One prominent New Zealand cricket player confided to our Sports Policy Committee that, while fielding, he constructed in his head an entire outdoor rockery. Another was able to complete a science degree by correspondence.

An attempt has been made to shorten the game down to an hour (with three fifteen-minute intervals) but purists argue that the game is completely altered by shortening it. The debate has raged on for years and no one cares.

The long and the short of it is that cricket is not a manly game. It is invariably called off when it rains – a decision which is the source of much merriment among people like myself who played rugby as a child in gale force southerlies on a rugby field constructed on the local rubbish tip! Cricket is cancelled over poor light for God's sake! Give them torches or miners' helmets and let them get on with it. Most of the audience are too pissed by nightfall to care.

And what do you make of a game where players are dismissed if they put their leg before the wicket?!! No wonder there's been massive confusion and a retreat to mind-altering substances. The game appears to be about defending the stumps. Some batsmen are even prepared to put their testicles (with the appropriate protection – which does raise questions about their commitment) on the line to protect those wickets. You should be able to lie, sit or persuade someone from the terraces to stand in front of them with his eyes closed!

In short, the game is best suited to the anally retentive. It should never have left England.

If I had my way, I'd introduce the one-over game, played under strobing lights. The players would be drug-tested along with the spectators. If either party was found to have more drugs than the other, they would be banned for life.

The stresses and strains of being a professional sportsperson are such that, sooner or later, athletes will be tempted to add meaning to their lives by experimenting with drugs.

This has been going on for years in Eastern Europe where children are torn from their mother's breast at three months and placed on intravenous steroids so that women turn into male shotputters and the other way round.

I could not condone performance-enhancing drugs (apart from possibly rhino horn and Viagra) but the temptation is understandable. How does it feel, for example, to be a swimmer doing backstroke for much of your professional career, watching the roofs of various swimming pools for hours and emerging with two goggle rings around the eyes?

How must it feel to be a synchronised swimmer, bobbing up and down with a clothes peg on your nose and seeing the pity in other people's eyes?!!

These people deserve our support – and all the drugs they can lay their wet hands on!

Australian administrators recently announced that ballroom dancers will be drug-tested.

Is this going too far?

The only significant ballroom dancing film was Marlon Brando's *Last Tango in Paris*. It was not a happy film in the sense that *Babe* was and the dancing (what there was of it) seemed to lead to sodomy and the abuse of one of this country's primary exports! Also, a cursory examination of the footage seems to indicate that women who do the tango develop unsightly long necks. (Maria Schneider was able to shoot and kill

Jonah – lucky enough to be standing at the right place at the right time.

Marlon Brando before she turned into an emu.)

People will indulge in all kinds of substances to embroider their everyday experiences. Sport is not an everyday experience and it would seem that drugs come into it when it moves beyond an idle pastime and develops significance. Significance must be avoided at all costs.

Britain's 80,000 pigeon-fanciers have been told by tax authorities that their interest is not a sport, on the grounds that the pigeon does all the work. Ballooning, baton-twirling and bowls, on the other hand, do earn tax exemptions as sports.

It's a matter of opinion whether a jockey does much in the scheme of things – apart from hang on, in the same way that luge riders in the Winter Olympics can only strap themselves in and hope for the best.

The test of individual effort is an inappropriate and limiting one in the world of sport and entertainment. Can Jonah Lomu be regarded as a sports hero simply because he is standing in position when someone else passes him the ball – while I am not because I was not there? How much of this is down to luck?

In Southland, a debate raged over whether or not a local darts player, Jill MacDonald, was entitled to a Sports Foundation grant. Opponents dismiss darts as a "sideshow activity" associated with pubs and drinking, rather than a real sport involving rigorous training schedules and careful attention to diet.

This narrow interpretation is typical of the puritanical view of sport. A pub is no less demanding a training ground than a modern gymnasium. Those who play darts develop muscular thumbs, fingers and drinking arms. There are no hamstring or niggling groin injuries but there have been instances where a dart has pierced an ear – no great problem in a game in which many are anaesthetised from the outset.

Some games have become less of a sport because of the application of new technology. The International Tennis Federation has been having a series of meetings to discuss why the rallies in modern tennis are so short.

The obvious answer is that hair gel doesn't take long to dry. But the new carbon-fibre racquets have something to do with it. A ball bouncing off one travels faster than the speed of light and it's only sheer chance that the player at the other end manages to touch it at all! The simple rule is: the better the equipment, the less enjoyable the game.

YOU SHOULD HAVE SEEN IT COMING YESTERDAY.

When rugby turned professional and live television coverage of the tests was handed over to the 207,000 clients of Sky television, the Rugby Union and the players' representatives told the people of New Zealand that we "should have known" that the eventual downstream consequences were likely to be live coverage for only a few paying customers.

Stupid! Stupid! Stupid!

Perhaps we were preoccupied at the time by violence in the game.

There was Richard Loe applying the eye to the finger and Robin Brooke getting off a punching incident on the grounds of provocation (name-calling?), an "improved disciplinary record" (hadn't punched many people lately) and the fact that the punch didn't connect (phew!). No wonder O.J. Simpson originally asked to have his case heard before the Rugby Union's disciplinary committee!

Johan le Roux was pilloried by the international media and sent home in disgrace because he tried to nibble Sean Fitzpatrick's ear. Admittedly, the rugby field is not a good place for men to display affection but given the amount of hugging and hand-holding we have seen in recent years, did it really matter?

Leaving aside a more mature and affectionate approach to the game, there can be few Kiwis over the age of fourteen who have not set the alarm for a 2 a.m. callout, where bleary eyed and cocoa in hand, we have sat bolt upright, fast asleep, watching a test match against South Africa. The experience is part of our national culture – as Kiwi as holding a tranny to your ear to hear a rugby match during a poorly timed wedding.

The monetarists have so far been unable to lay a hand on the game. Scoping studies were carried out looking at reducing the number of players (getting rid of dead wood like the props but keeping the Number Eight on the grounds that any man who is prepared to put his shoulders to another man's buttocks . . . well . . . needs friends!).

The game appears to have defied the new economic climate and gone from strength to strength. The Super 12 competition has meant that nearly everyone needing a job in the game has one and at the end of their playing careers, when they are completely knackered, they can still play overseas.

It could be argued that the country needs a national game which is more within reach of everyman and everywoman – people who are not able to train every day and develop protective layers of muscle.

Lawn bowls is an obvious choice. It already has a huge following, the right mix of social and sporting skills and a goodly amount of humour. The inventor of the game designed a ball which is too heavy on one side – the end result being that when you throw it, it careens all over the bloody place!

The aim apparently ("aim" being a moot point – there's nothing you can do with the bloody thing other than let it go and hope that it doesn't swerve onto the motorway and take out a Morris 1100 full of badminton players) is to try and strike a ball called Jack. If you do hit Jack and knock him into the ditch, then it's hoorays all the way round and a shout from the joker who brought Jack along.

Lawn bowls has also led to the kind of rough play which would have done Richard Loe proud. One bowler called another a "fat pig" and clocked him with a bowl. In another incident in the National Championships in Dunedin, one contestant threw the black bowl so hard it caused the aforementioned Jack to leap up and KO a bloke down the far end. He slumped onto the green like one of Tua's hand-picked favourites.

All in all, the game's a joy! Because of the amount of piss-drinking involved, Jonah Lomu wouldn't even need a driving licence. He could share the shuttle bus with everyone else.

In the main though, with bowls there is not the injury rate (apart from death from natural causes) that you find in rugby.

Professional rugby players have their own ACC agent!

When you consider that pro rugby carries with it the certainty of being hurt, why does Joe Blow, the ordinary taxpayer, have to fork out for All Black injuries?

Would you attempt to tackle Jonah? Of course not. If you did, you would not deserve ACC on the grounds that you knowingly took the risk. You would be justified (and taxpayers would be grateful) in creeping up on Jonah from behind and laying him out with a length of galvanised pipe!

We'll liven up the game of bowls a tad. Bowlers will be permitted under special circumstances (ie, if they want to) to pick up the bowl and run with it. Four points for a touchdown and two if they manage to boot it through the clubhouse window. One day not too far from now we will see Jonah storm over the try line, fifteen bowlers in white clinging to his arms and legs.

Let's be honest — we like it when it hurts!

If you look for a common thread in what Kiwis enjoy most about sport, the answer would be horrendous crashes. The series of Minties advertisements featuring people injuring themselves while playing sport has been very popular. They reflect our respect for people who do dangerous things in the name of sport and our resentment at their success.

Great moments in sport include:
1) The LA Olympics — Zola Budd ankle-taps Mary Decker.
2) The NZ Commonwealth Games — the Scottish diver, who on the metre-high diving board lands on his own head on the end of the diving board.
3) The recent track and field meet in Europe where a javelin-thrower finally impaled an official.
4) The Winter Olympics where, time after time, Norwegian skiers land astride Norfolk pines.
5) Turkish rower Ali Bilal falling out of his boat and being rescued by a launch.
6) Italian long-distance runner Dorandi Pietri who, in 1908, stumbled into the arena at the end of his marathon, collapsed six times on his final lap and was disqualified because he ran around the arena the wrong way!
7) American ice skater Tonya Harding arranging to have one of her opponents knee-capped. (A recent television special boasted "39 Living Legends on Ice". Not one, not 38 – but 39! And Tonya Harding wasn't one of them.)
8) In a desire to liven up the America's Cup, the Aussies pull the plug on their boat.

Sadly, not all sports are capable of such interesting moments. What can be done about such dull (from a spectator's point of view) sports as swimming? Danyon Loader seems to be a nice (although uncommunicative) chap. But then he spends a lot of time staring at the bottom of a swimming pool! No wonder he is so resentful.

Swimmers must be able to change lanes without warning. Instead of the present clumsy starting system, where people invariably jump in too soon and upset all the others, officials should step up and push the contestants in without warning.

Gymnastics used to be dull apart from the uneven bars. A Kiwi, Sarah Thompson, even won a silver in the event. They should introduce a judder bar event and something rather dirty with tassles, in a public bar.

We're approaching the millennium – get sexy or get out!

One of the cruel and unsettling aspects of life is change. None of us wants it because when things stay the way they are you can usually find your socks in the hot water cupboard.

Change has absolutely nothing going for it. The only people who want to change things are the people who want to make a buck. According to one English business survey, the new information technologies are actually costing businesses more time ("Come and show me how to work this, Susan") and the paperless office is generating more paper than ever before.

Sport used to be ours but it is not anymore. So we have to keep inventing more, even sillier games, to stay ahead of Rupert Murdoch and the people who own the teams.

I see the future of sport. It will involve a meeting down an alleyway between Rupert Murdoch and a one-legged, blind, hopscotch player. Rupert will pause for a moment, chequebook in hand, then turn and walk away, a broken man.

synchronised swimming – a sign of how desperate some people are to conform.

Th Envi

e

ronment

If ever there was an overplayed word in the world, it is the "environment". The concept is far too broad. It apparently stretches from horizon to horizon. Consequently, there is no need for the kind of intellectual rigour fifth formers would normally bring to other subjects. If, for example, you are going to "save the environment", what are you going to save it in?

Answer: the environment.

Thus we have an environment full of environment, a bucket full of a bucket, a handful full of a handful.

It doesn't make sense.

And what the hell is a carbon sink?

The companies which extract natural gas and oil from the ground are now required to plant trees to balance out the carbon dioxide which may one day be released as a result of their activities.

When I die, I too will release carbon dioxide, although not as much as a methanol plant. In a momentary desire to please the greenies, I wrote into my last will and testament (although it won't be my last because I argue with people and keep changing the beneficiary of my Billy Bunter book collection) that in keeping with the carbon sink policy, three pines should be planted at my graveside.

Hills. Aren't they just the same everywhere?

You can imagine my horror when later research showed that when those trees come to maturity and are felled and turned into a dozen kidney-shaped coffee tables (also laid down in my will) the manufacturing process will release the same amount of carbon dioxide! In other words, the sink will not result in the offensive carbon dioxide being contained, or sunk. It will merely hang about waiting to be released on another date.

Why did I bother? (And I shan't now. I will have my body – once rigor mortis has set in – turned directly into a kidney-shaped table.)

This is a fine example of the pseudo-science and half-baked ideas which bedevil the green movement.

Animal flatulence is responsible for holes in the ozone layer. There was a lot of nonsense put about that it had something to do with the foam in the back of old fridges. Who could possibly believe such a thing? Can you imagine a meeting of boffins somewhere, studying a map of the sky with large holes in it.

"Good God!" one of them says. "How are we going to explain this away?"

Just then, another scientist is removing a pottle of yoghurt (Pottle? Pottle? If we can find the person who invented that word, we'll be able to solve a lot of our problems!) from a tired old fridge humming quietly to itself in the corner of the room.

"I know," says the pottle-puncher, "let's say that hundreds of thousands of tired old fridges all over the world are responsible."

"You beauty!" cry the others, and a myth is born.

The idea catches on for a time because every householder is familiar with the mysterious pool of water (first put down to cat urination) which forms at the back of the fridge. For years we simply wiped it up. Now it takes on a sinister meaning. Watch out for that leaky stuff. It causes the hole in the ozone layer!

Small children are forced to wear layers of greasy suntan lotion which gets in their eyes and makes them cry. They, in turn, come to look at the little old fridge in the family bach as an enemy to mankind and won't go near it. Sometimes they kick it when no one is looking. Eventually, the little old fridge is put on a hire trailer with a lot of other household refuse and taken to the tip, where it lies on its back, bent and useless, looking at all the other little fridges, saying what did we do??

Cows: Farm animals about to launch an attack on the ozone layer.

Putting the blame on animal farts is a much easier concept to sell. Farm animals are known to be noisy, smelly and likely to unload their waste products without ceremony. But, again, the scientists made a mistake when they identified methane from animal flatulence as the reason for the problem. Methane sounds okay. It almost sounds useful.

Environmentalists almost invariably have two agendas. One is to save the world. The second is to pay us back!

The greenies will take advantage of this. They will say:
- animal waste products must be recycled.
- why waste valuable methane gas?
- let's force motorists (who are using up the world's resources at a disproportionate rate, damaging the environment, etc etc) to park in service station forecourts, back a cattlebeast up to the opening to the petrol tank and feed it grass until it fills the tank.

There is something about the upbringing of your average environmentalist which instils a polite desire to seek revenge. On behalf of the giant weta. How do we explain this?

The profile of the average greenie shows someone who was unexceptional at school, polite, hair neatly combed in the mornings.

Unexceptional at sport, usually caught in the second run at bullrush, always did their homework with very tidy drawings – even when no drawings were required.

They did not receive the rewards they felt they were due! This translates in later life to a stern desire to lecture and admonish from the high ground.

It's very hard to argue with someone who wants to save a native parrot – even though the parrot is too stupid to save itself.

Take the case of the kakapo or one of the other "K" birds, which are, we are told, rapidly dwindling in number. I have no idea how they estimate the numbers. These parrots are subject to a lot of attention and counting. By now they are probably census-shy. It wouldn't surprise me if, when they hear the approach of Roman sandals, they duck down into bunkers where they will never be found.

It is not uncommon for scientists to attach cameras to these "endangered species" when they do find them, then act surprised when the birds do not mate!

There are some people (politicians and rock stars) who enjoy filming their own sexual exploits. But the kakapo has a low libido at the best of times. They are frequently interrupted in the act by Statistics New Zealand! No wonder the poor parrot can't enjoy a bit of legover and has almost given up the whole idea.

This was confirmed last summer when DOC cleared an island of rats so that one eligible female and four males birds in their prime could do their thing.

The *New Zealand Herald* reported that the males "failed to boom"! No wonder. All that pressure to perform! It is hard to tell what makes a female kakapo eligible or even attractive. Maybe she was unapproachable in that pursed (beaked?) lipped kind of way that some women have when they know they are sought after?

The failure of the liaison was all for the best.

Inevitably the film of the act would find its way onto the internet under "parrot-porn".

I don't want to be seen as an "environment-basher", a soccer hooligan to the natural world. It is more that I am concerned about stress levels.

Road rage is not simply about motorists who cut you off. It is the culmination of computers which "go down", telephone messages which keep you on hold and the whole edifice of monetarism and the free market which is making us a nation of mean-minded, desperate, dob-a-dole-bludger, Third World coolies.

I am worried about your amygdala.

Or more precisely, I am worried about the recently discovered direct access to the amygdala which causes it to flood. This may not sound serious if you are still reading this. Normally messages to the brain pass through the frontal lobes where thinking and judgment takes place.

The "No, I won't eat this kakapo because someone may be watching me" part of the brain.

A new message pathway, recently discovered, enables messages to charge straight to the amygdala which makes you impulsive: "I WILL eat this bloody kakapo because that booming noise reminds me of Mum basting a chook!"

A flooded amygdala is more dangerous than a flooded Waikato.

So it's time we loosened up on the environment. We have enough to get flooded about. Our own version of the Gulf War – the carpet bombing of the tussock moth – caused great distress among the residents of Auckland. It is to be hoped that the T Moth has been constrained (why didn't they just light a big candle on the top of One Tree Hill?) But chances are, it has not. If it has, something else will turn up to worry us.

The discovery of fireblight by a Kiwi scientist in Melbourne (that same fireblight which has kept New Zealand exports out of Australia) nearly caused a war with them across the ditch!

Small bugs just are. They exist in the same unfair way that science has discovered that pretty women and handsome men are more likely to have higher IQs.

There is no way you can say this is fair. It is appalling to think that Pamela Anderson and Helena Bonham Carter are brainy as well.

The scientists in this case don't say "beautiful" or "good-looking". They talk about faces being symmetrical or asymmetrical. "Men with symmetrical faces have more sex partners, begin sex earlier in life and engage in more sexual infidelity."

Take a look in the mirror and if you find a lopsided face looking back at you, or only one ear, chances are you are stupid as well (for looking in the mirror).

Life is quite clearly not fair and contending with this unfairness requires effort enough. Burdening yourself with worries about the environment could be the last straw.

There is a school of thought which argues that we have an affinity and therefore a source of sustenance among creatures who are mammals.

Is it possible that in emotional or spiritual terms, we can get a dividend from caring about them? Are they worth the investment?

Well, they may have been once. The whole history of human and dolphin is well recorded on cracked Roman and Grecian urns. A couple of Greek saucers have been unearthed in a garage sale which show dolphins named Hector tossing babies into the air. Dolphins were used as nannies in those days until it was shown that immigrants without work permits could be more dangerous.

Hector dolphins were shown to be particularly adept at playing with infants. As so often is the case, there was a great deal more to the story than popular belief suggests. Dolphins drop more babies in a passing situation than they catch. Using computer-aided graphics on possession versus handling errors, dolphins actually come in behind the England A rugby team.

In June 1998, a report was released which sent shivers down the spines of childcare agencies. There is evidence that dolphins kill their young.

Researchers for the Whale and Dolphin Conservation Society (good on them for their integrity!) said five of eight bottlenose dolphin calves found dead on the northeast coast of Scotland between 1992 and 1996 had injuries consistent with attacks by other bottlenoses. (They had been "bottled". Had they died as the result of a Liverpool kiss, there would have been more bruising across the bridge of the nose.)

Is the bottlenose dolphin exceptional? Only insofar as whales travel in a pod, most dolphins in a school but the bottlenose in a six-pack.

What on earth would possess women to trust their babies in dolphin pools?

We must remember that we have only recently emerged from the seventies and eighties, when the stoned philosophies of the sixties started to harden and worm their way into popular thought.

In the sixties, whole communes of people gathered around and chanted (they couldn't remember individual words) while mothers gave birth. One brain surgeon seconded to a commune had the idea that properly heated bathwater could approximate the fluid in the womb.

Nobody thought to speculate about why it is that babies want to leave the bathwomb. Nine months with only the squishy bass line of the mother's heart playing is long enough!

Books were published on handmade paper suggesting, nay, decreeing, that the child would benefit from escaping from one bath into another. The first thing many of these babies saw was a flannel – which is why they now dress in the manner of the Generation X-er.

Tim Shadbolt lived in a car packing case in a commune for a number of years and has many funny stories to tell about it. Most of the people who tried it became disillusioned and all that remains are the women who still tie their greying hair back and smell of goat's milk.

The Earth Mother predated the Unhappy Woman by less than ten years.

The Unhappy Man followed five or six years after the Unhappy Woman (dealt with adequately in the chapter, "Everything You Will Ever Need to Know about Men and Women") but note the exponential growth in unhappiness.

Exponentiality may be one of the most important concepts never before coined in a word. What it means in simple terms is if your Holden costs $200 to repair today, your Toyota will cost you a grand.

Or from the bloke who owns the garage who used to be your friend: "If I were you, mate, I'd buy a new one!"

Planned obsolescence was an expression which shocked us twenty-five years ago but which is an obsolescent expression today. We have no ongoing relationship with vacuum cleaners (the Hoover or the Electrolux), fridges, radios, cars, clothes (one good suit, sensible shoes), gloves or a hat. The modern stereo with CD player and a thousand virtues stands or sits in the corner of a room, like the kind of machine you could sterilise surgical instruments in. Given that modern music is often manufactured, teased, enhanced by computer effects, perhaps that is appropriate.

God is not in the machine!

Where is the love, the hope, the connection with adventures present and past? (I know that this is the kind of talk that makes underwater-hockey-players-turned-chief-executives roll their cute little eyes. They find attraction repellent. Change is the only constant, they say, slapping their flippers together. The rest of us then have to wait until the trainer throws them a fish.)

In the absence of things we can adhere to, it is little wonder that we are obsessed with the thought that we can relate to the whale. We cannot harpoon them now, except for the Japanese. (We cannot harpoon Japanese – even for the purpose of scientific experiments.)

Whenever a **whale** goes ashore in Aotearoa, hundreds of willing volunteers turn out to mind them through the change of tide.

We do not know why it is that whales, complete with their own enormously efficient internal navigation systems, hit the beach. A bad night on the krill? Or perhaps it is a perfectly normal response to a lifetime of being a whale?

Whatever the reason, they suddenly get it into their heads to head for the mountains. They do this in the expectation that they will be saved.

In the same way that the government expresses concern about welfare dependency, so the whale has come to expect the New Zealand shoreline to be like Club Med for whales. Once aground, they expect to be patted and pampered until the tide returns. Frequently they come back for seconds. This costs money.

The time spent by the average citizen donning a wetsuit which is too small for them has increased from just under fifteen minutes to one hour and a quarter (getting it off takes longer).

If you also took into account the real cost of urination in the wetsuit on the environment, then the whole whale-saving thing becomes a marginal exercise, economically speaking. Realistically, we would be better to mount harpoons on the sandhills and conduct a little Japanese science.

The earlier chapter on the economy indicated that time on the beach is no longer a priority. All of our recreational and social activities must now be measured with a view to their true cost.

Why do we look for

trampers?

The ones that get lost. (Although searches get underway for trampers who are then found – making them not lost. We can only really find out if trampers are lost by leaving them there.)

This is probably the right idea. Surely part of the thrill of tramping is that you may never see your loved ones again? For the family too, there is the awe and respect that they will have when daddy-with-the-three-day-growth-and-bad-body-odour turns up again in the living room!

What a wonderful opportunity for renewed appreciation of the family! If on the other hand, you get lost in the bush — tough scroggin!

In the *Heartland* programme entitled "Life and Death in the Waimarino", I carried a dead pig on my back. In a race. Now why would anyone want to do that? Well, to start with, many New Zealanders still identify with hunting and killing. Prestige comes with the kill. Carrying the pig (or deer) out of the bush is part of the exercise. I never knew that. I got dragged into carrying the pig for the worst of reasons – the crowd called for me to do it. Because people think that television is a prissy job and that people on it are sissies until they prove themselves to be otherwise.

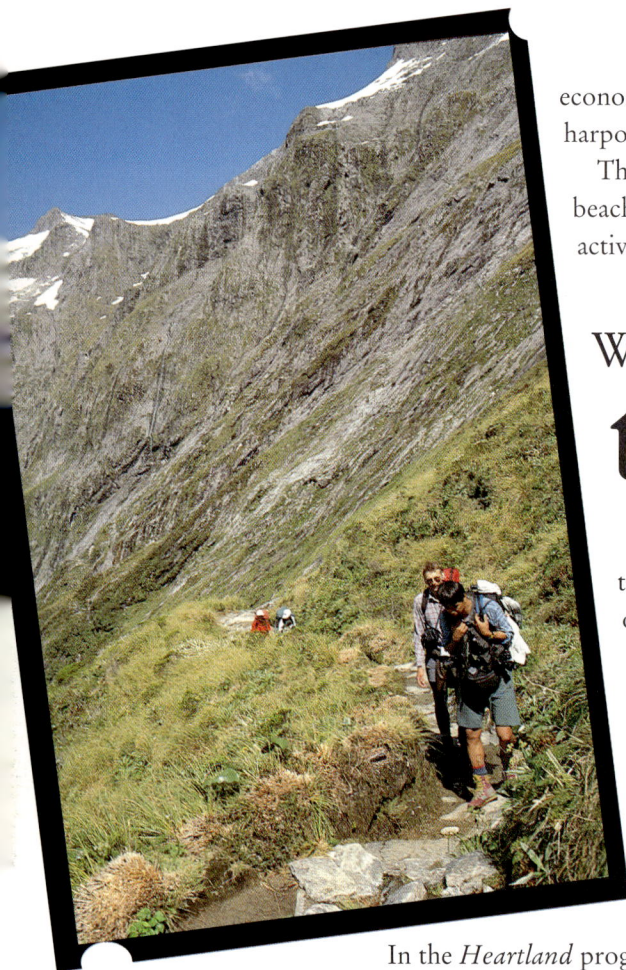

Trampers: sad people who can't scrape up a bus fare.

So I carry a dead and bleeding (down the back of my shirt) pig, ride bucking bronco machines (West Coast), ride horses down rivers (they fall over), do cycle trips, go up the Routeburn Track, climb Mt Ruapehu (in summer) and do countless other silly things which I have no business doing.

I even allowed the police at the Marlborough A&P Show to persuade me to be chased by a police dog and brought to the ground – with a thump! My shoulder has not healed nine months later.

Depending on your definition, I will always be a phoney. I try these things because I want to know what other people get out of it. For me, it is a second-hand experience.

A revealing moment in the life of a television star – forced to perform an ugly indecent act, in order to be noticed.

I was comforted to read in the biography of comedian Peter Cook (by Harry Thompson) that one of the driving forces behind his more destructive impulses (he drank himself to death) was his low boredom threshold. I know what that is like (the low boredom threshold, not the drinking yourself to death – so far). The nature rambles I am forced to undertake have some use. They give me time to think about more exciting things. In itself, I find all that bush-walk stuff boring.

From time to time there is an ugly clash of worlds, when I have to interview someone about nature in a natural setting. One such person was David Miller in his

home, the legendary "Paradise" near Glenorchy. He had previously been interviewed by *Country Calendar* and possibly had some reservations about going through the whole business again.

Being universally admired by the "green" brigade, he behaved like a bit of a lead singer himself. I waited outside his house while director Bruce Morrison spent two hours trying to persuade him to guide us through the bush and identify the local mountains.

After the first hour, I was all for bailing out. If people choose not to be filmed – good on them! It's only television. David did eventually emerge and up into the hills we went. He is a canny chap and sensed my huge lack of interest in the minutiae of bush life and proceeded to ask me schoolteacherly-type questions while the cameras rolled: "Do you see anything different about these trees?" "Name three common fungi found in the bush."

He sensed that the very thought of fungi reduced me to tears of frustration and boredom and that being treated like a third former made me squirm. I suspect he enjoyed every moment of it.

My director, Bruce Morrison, who is something of a sage in these matters (see the earlier chapter "So Why Were You Born?") believes that I avoid situations where I can confront myself.

It is true that if ever you were going to meet yourself, **unarmed** and with no backup, the bush would be the place to do it.

I went up the Routeburn Track for the *Holiday* programme. We travelled by

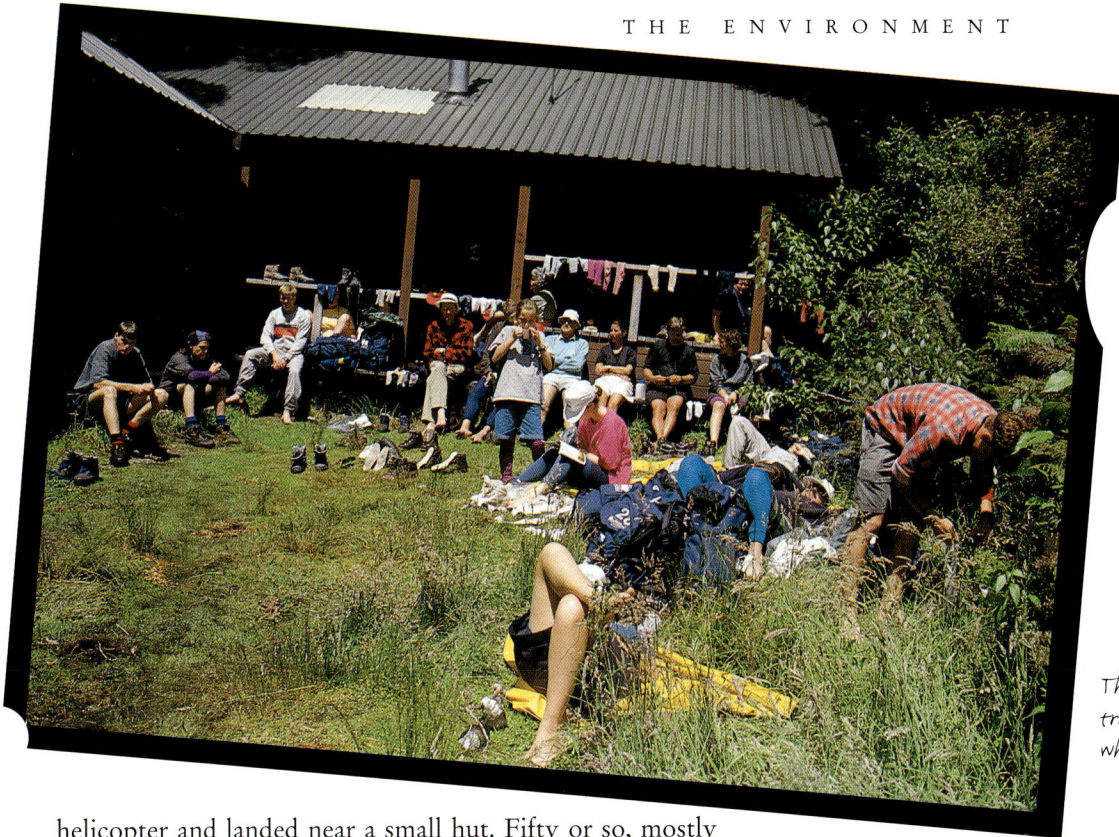

This is what trampers look like when they nest.

helicopter and landed near a small hut. Fifty or so, mostly
overseas visitors, came out and waved (or so I thought) but it turned out the rotor wash
had blown away their sleeping bags and socks. They disliked me from the outset. I
didn't like them either. I actually heard some of them complaining that I kept them
awake in the hut because I snored! Don't they snore in Germany?

It was so bloody boring! Most of my stimulus comes from individuals – interesting,
different people. But the bush . . . it's so . . . uniformly . . . green! Birds making noises
and waterfalls. You can see those at home.

If the Victoria University Tramping Club and all of the people from Germany who
have never seen trees want to go outdoors – fine. But it won't be our national religion
if I have anything to do with it and all those pursed-lipped, scroggin-munching, hairy-
legged outdoors folk better learn to find their own way home!

An *Econo*

Named

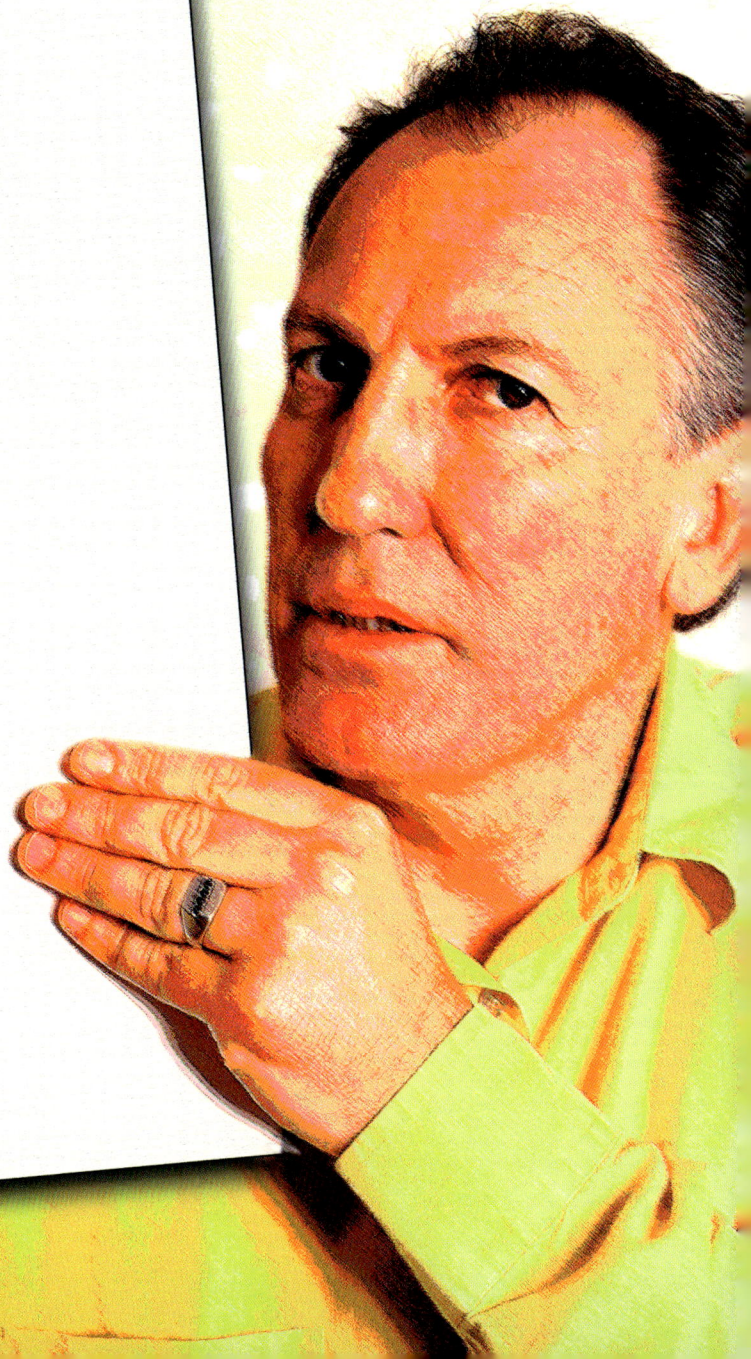

my
Belinda

Up until 1922, **there was no economy**. In the same way that until quite recently there was no environment, only hills and rivers.

Our parents and grandparents went to work. They didn't even know they were employed! Many of our forebears managed to avoid the economy altogether. Things started to go wrong about twenty years ago.

With the rise of the university-educated classes, a demand arose for jobs to put them in where they wouldn't hurt anybody. Heavy earthmoving machinery was obviously out of the question along with most occupations which demanded dexterity, physical exertion and the ability to hammer a straight nail into a piece of wood.

Social work was invented, along with statistics and economics.

Of the three, economics seemed least likely to catch on because it was practically useless. People like Keynes and George Bernard Shaw (who hated it and went back to being Irish) flirted with it for a time, piling unlikely theory upon unlikely theory until the tang of bullshit hung heavy in the air.

The Second World War kicked the whole game along. A shell-shocked population wanted to know what the dickens was going on and the brainy kids saw their chance. They would insist that a knowledge of economics would prevent any further periods of uncertainty and insecurity.

These are the people who predicted that New Zealand farmers and exporters would be better off once the dollar fell – only commodity prices fell at the same rate. They didn't know that the Asian financial crisis was about to happen, or that Japan would sink into recession. They tell us the current account deficit is our fault because we buy houses to live in. Winston Peters tells us off for not saving. (He has been unable to save personally because he is in litigation with a lot of people. You only have the excuse that you don't have any money left over to save.)

The terrible truth about the economy is that it is impossible to manage. It is not a graph or a set of statistics. It is a human being.

The economy's real name

is Belinda.

Reputed to be the home of Belinda the economy.

She lives in a small, well-appointed apartment on The Terrace in Wellington.

On first meeting her, it is surprising how petite she really is. Well-groomed, it is the flash of red on the fingernails and lips which give her away.

"I love to perform!" she says, with the coquettish tone of one who is used to getting her way.

Her critics say she is too small for the part but she shrugs that off.

"When you consider how fast I have to move – up and down – it wouldn't do to be any larger than I am."

But wouldn't a bit of fat be welcomed by her followers?

"There's no fat here," she says, squeezing her waistline playfully.

For a long time, she went out with a guy with the un-Kiwi name of Harvard, who worked for First Boston. Rumour has it that she is still seeing him but she denies it.

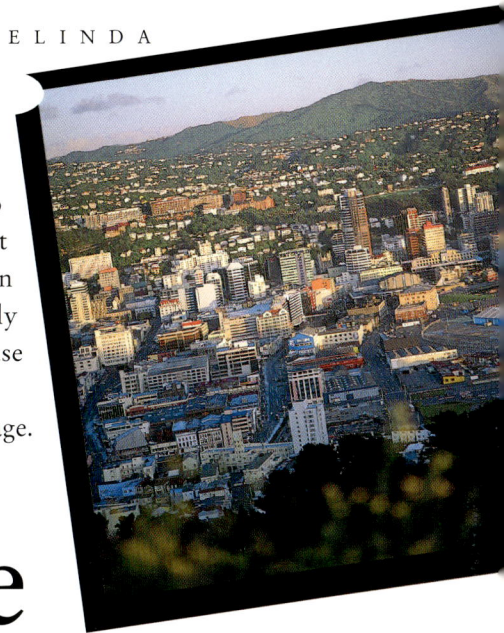

Her beau was something of a "monetarist" – meaning that he danced with both legs held tightly together.

"He got . . . well . . . boring."

But the eyes reveal a flicker of doubt.

There was undoubtedly pressure from other members of the family, many of whom are not well off. As observers of the US economy (real name: Hank) have noted, sooner or later the poor relations move in for their share and trash the place. They don't understand that you can get three million to leave Brierleys and 1.7 mill for running the nation's telephone exchange because you can't put a price on managerial responsibility — so it might as well be a big one!

The poor just don't get it. So they get angry and look for simple solutions. Could it be that Belinda is worried that, like Mussolini's girlfriend, she might end up hanging with the wrong crowd?

To be fair to her, she is only a frontperson for the Reserve Bank Act, which says (and I quote): "No matter if, or when, you think you are going to get ahead, you won't. We'll see to it."

The country is run with the aid of a monetary conditions index, which saves the government from having to run the country. The net effect is like having to count on pocket money from the wet, dermatitis-ridden hands of a capricious mother.

> To sum up Belinda's situation:
> ● you can date her
> ● blow in her ear
> ● pay the fines on her overdue videos . . . but in terms of a dividend, you might as well believe they'll bring back Buck Shelford!

Any lucky break for the wage-earner in New Zealand will come about not because of any management of the economy, it will be because of a windfall like the AMP shares or the recent discovery of gas and oil deposits on the East Coast. Those East Coast oil sediments came about because a whole lot of plankton fell dead on the ocean floor 53 million years ago!

Now what are the chances of that happening again? Not very great. But even that is no cause for alarm. When we are siphoning the last drops of "Plankton Premium" into the tank, something else will turn up.

It always does.

Don't worry. Be happy.

An Ode to Club Sandwiches
By Gary McCormick

O February the unkind month
Of heartache, heat & drought
Why leave the house, why breathe at all
Tho thin-sliced's not about

In footy clubs and RSA's
Across our native land
They're taking in the tablecloths
And packing up the band

In tennis clubs they're dressed in black
And bridge will not be played
In Parliament the government
Can but rue the day
When the white and thinly sliced
Finally went away

It was not so much the bread itself
Which did not make the cut
But the plate which dare not speak his name
A sandwich called the "The Club"

This multi-layered treasure chest
Of tuna, greens and cheese
Once filled the gobs of kings & queens
And brought them to their knees

At wedding feasts, dear Auntie Flo
Could dance till 4.00 a.m.
With little else for comfort
Than 3 clubbies and a gin

And Uncle Pat, the day he died
Asked for one more bite
Of a sammy down the rugby club
They brought him on that night

And now the bit he could not chew
Remains there under glass
With Sean Fitzpatrick's rugby boot
And other body parts

They all stood at the basin
And hung their heads in shame
For the clubbies that had left them
All had to take the blame

When it comes to sound the call
And tell their grandkids yet
Of all the tricks God placed upon
This generation's heads

They'll try to overlook the one
Which cut them to the quick
A plate stacked high with sandwiches
Each several inches thick

A symphony in sandwich-style
A mighty, three-packed play
A cake of a sort, without sugar or salt
A monument to taste.

Present,

But

CHAPTER 9

Not
Involved

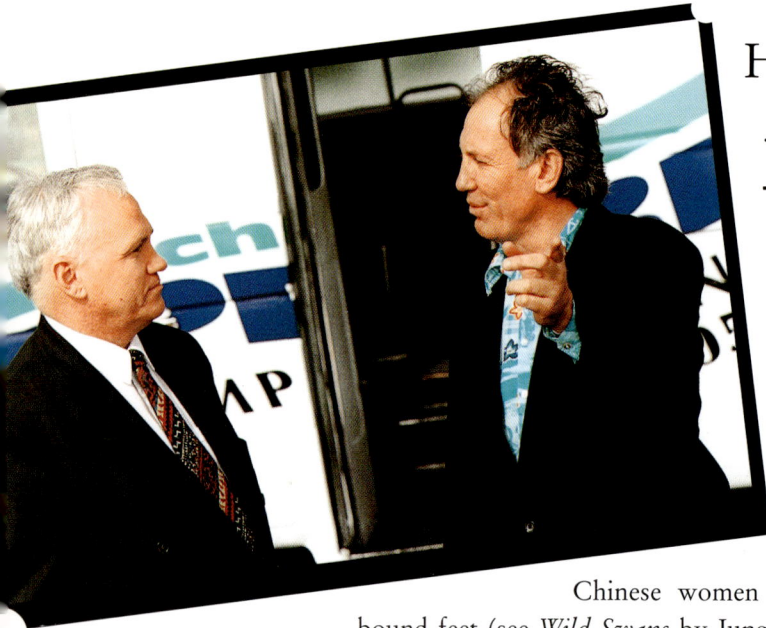

How do you avoid a
major
crisis in your life?

You can't. Our lives today are a minefield of psychic explosions. To walk through it relatively unscathed (which is to say with minor burns and shrapnel wounds, rather than a leg blown off) you have to maintain a sense of perspective.

Chinese women walk hundreds of kilometres with painfully bound feet (see *Wild Swans* by Jung Chang.) The North Vietnamese survive carpet bombing. Lightly dressed, poorly armed North Koreans take on the might of the American military machine and win. Students are gunned down in Tiananmen Square. People starve to death all over Africa.

My generation was lucky enough to avoid being conscripted into a war. Generation X managed to avoid anti-war protests. Arthur Harawira is forced to fight actors pretending to be Portuguese soldiers at a book launch!

If this keeps up, the disaffected will be forced to assault authors who may be thinking about writing a screenplay in which Martians may kidnap someone no one even cares about!

Grievances of this calibre are the product of a blur between fantasy and reality brought about by an under-utilised brain.

The brain is a remarkable organ with a mind of its own. Obsessive people understand this. They are driven to turning light switches on and off, going back and checking the

"ACT leader Richard Prebble has confirmed the taxpayer-funded parliamentary office of ACT list MP Owen Jennings was used for a meeting to promote a get-rich scheme this month. But despite Mr Jennings being present, he was not involved, Mr Prebble said today."

— Evening Post, May 1998.

iron a dozen times, etc etc, because they can't find enough to think about to occupy the 70 per cent of unused space in the spongy grey area.

This big space can be very tricky. Like any big space, it is a natural source of concern to Westerners. If we see one, we build a shopping mall or a car park on it. We know that if it is left to its own devices it will sprout weeds and car wrecks will be dumped there.

The wind will howl over it at night and the homeless will move in.

We won't be able to control it.

A lot of self-improvement books talk about this desire to control everything. They call people like us "control freaks".

We control freaks accept that being called names is part of the deal. We are called upon to make the decisions that keep things ticking over. Some of the tick-ees react by suggesting that there is something wrong with *us*.

There is nothing wrong with us, or there wouldn't be if you weren't such hopeless bastards!

Is it too much to ask that you don't run out of **toilet paper**, that socks are kept in matching pairs, or that the matchbox isn't full of dead matches??!!

And who will do the washing, put petrol in the car and vote for the go-ahead political parties – if we don't?

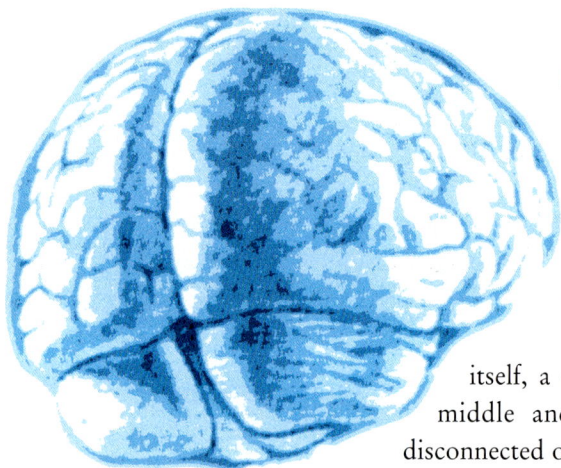

It's all very well for you to say, "Don't get so uptight." But the history of the world shows that the uptight people get things done. The others, who go along for the ride, deride the efforts of their champions and complain when social organisation breaks down.

We obsessive people get no satisfaction, so we turn to books to try to shut the world out. It's easier for both sides that way.

(When an obsessive brain finally breaks down trying to justify itself, a cyclone-type effect develops in which neurons spin into the middle and are gradually sucked out through the vortex. A few disconnected ones turn up later on the phone to Radio Pacific.)

This large carpark area of the brain acts as a stage for dust eddies. Phantoms materialise, swirl about and disappear again. Sometimes it gets so boring that people resort to drugs and alcohol to make it more interesting.

Marcus Lush (*Sunday News* exclusive, June 14, 1998) booked into an $800-a-day clinic to "dry out". His friends said, "At least Marcus has the courage to face up to the problem."

Wouldn't it be cheaper to run away?

There are two ways of handling problems. One is to confess, "hang it all out", seek professional guidance and admit to yourself that you're only human.

The other is to keep on running, at least until the last possible moment when the blue Pontiac you hadn't even noticed comes bearing down on top of you. That's what Dennis Hopper and Keith Richards did. They've never looked better.

The trick is in knowing exactly when to jump.

Let's face it, a life of chastity and self-discipline is not one that anyone other than an underwater hockey player would contemplate. Publicity-wise, you get no thanks for it.

At the funeral, they don't stand up and say, "Old Al was a lovely guy. He was the sort of guy who . . . well . . . yes, he was the kind of regular, decent person who never caused . . . who never did . . . never . . . Well, he just never, that's all."

No one would remember to turn up for a funeral like that. Even television evangelists like Oral Roberts get caught with their pants down sometimes, just to show that they are human enough to use the congregation's money to pay for sex.

Stay with human weakness for as long as you can, because

a) it's the most fun; and

b) people love a loser who is trying to do good, more than they love a goody-goody who is just . . . well . . . good!

The world is designed to wear us down like sea-water against stone.

That's why they invented the equator, different currencies, plastic packaging you can't open, exercise, coathangers attached to the wardrobe in upmarket hotels, noisy fan heaters, high-heeled shoes, wasabi, Mormons, check-in times, skinheads, the noise that vacuum cleaners make, born-again Christians, Arthur Harawira, hot dry nor-westers, lifts which break down, five-minute parking zones and Pauline Hanson.

These things don't happen by chance. They are all linked in some as yet undefined pattern.

Marcus had to pay $800 a day in a hospital where you start out "sleeping in a dormitory and doing the cleaning. To encourage bonding and team-building."

Now, I'm sorry. When the day comes for me to seek help, I won't be "mucking in" with the other losers. For $800 I expect to buy a small team, not build one.

I'm not one of the team.

Team-talk is big business these days. There are conferences held about it, motivational speakers and senior executives who peer about, looking to see who isn't

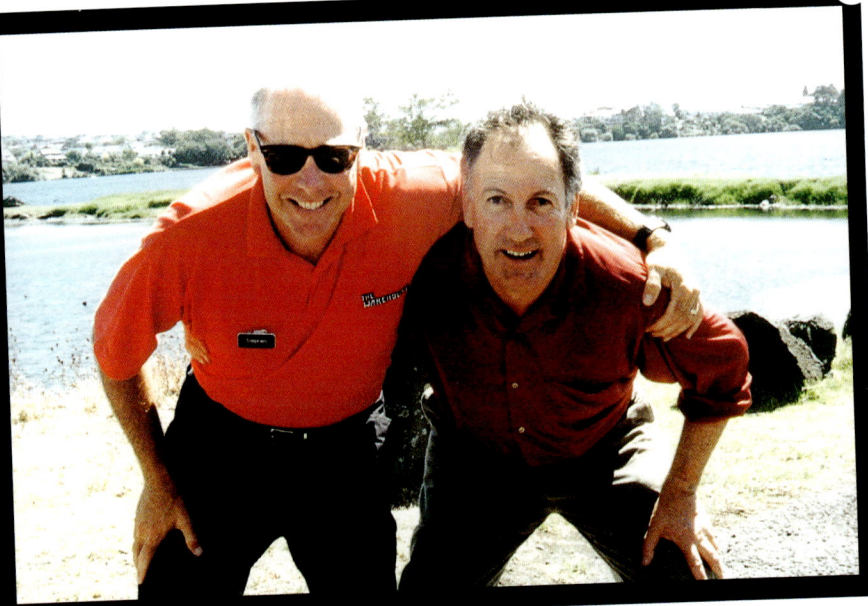

Stephen Tindall and the author hunker down to prepare for the new age of business.

in the team. Most large businesses (with the exception of Stephen Tindall at The Warehouse) encourage men to wear uniforms (suits) and the whole, grim, male hierarchical structure is still very much in evidence.

Former MP Michael Laws in his book on politics (which was issued and reissued because the sticker over the private parts kept falling off) refers to the climate of bullying. A former speaker of the House of Representatives has, with three of his colleagues, issued a report lamenting the behaviour in Parliament as being similar to that of competing boys' gangs.

The only way out of a climate of group bullying and pressure is the stand of the individual.

Teams are picked for games. If the game you've elected to play is that of being in a team, well and good. If it turns out that you are coerced or are simply expected to be in the team, tell them to go to hell.

There are two types of people: the team player and the individual. Society as a whole backs the idea of the team, so the individual starts off at a disadvantage. Nothing that can't be rectifed, but many a good soloist has been pushed over the edge by the insistent demand to stay "on side".

Following a very interesting interview, that determined pugilist of the legal profession, Christopher Harder, faxed me the following excerpt from Nelson Mandela's inaugural speech:

> *"Our deepest fear is not that we are inadequate.*
> *Our deepest fear is that we are powerful beyond measure.*
> *It is our light, not our darkness that most frightens us.*
> *We ask ourselves, who am I to be brilliant, gorgeous, talented*
> *and fabulous?*
> *Actually, who are you not to be?*
> *You are a child of God.*
> *Your playing small doesn't serve the world.*
> *There's nothing enlightened about shrinking so that other people*
> *won't feel insecure around you.*
> *We were born to manifest the glory of God that is within us;*
> *it's in everyone!*
> *And as we let our own light shine, we unconsciously give*
> *other people*
> *permission to do the same.*
> *As we are liberated from our own fear*
> *our presence automatically liberates others."*

When they come down on you and expect you to be like them, remember the words of the great bard Richard Prebble:

"I am present, but not involved."

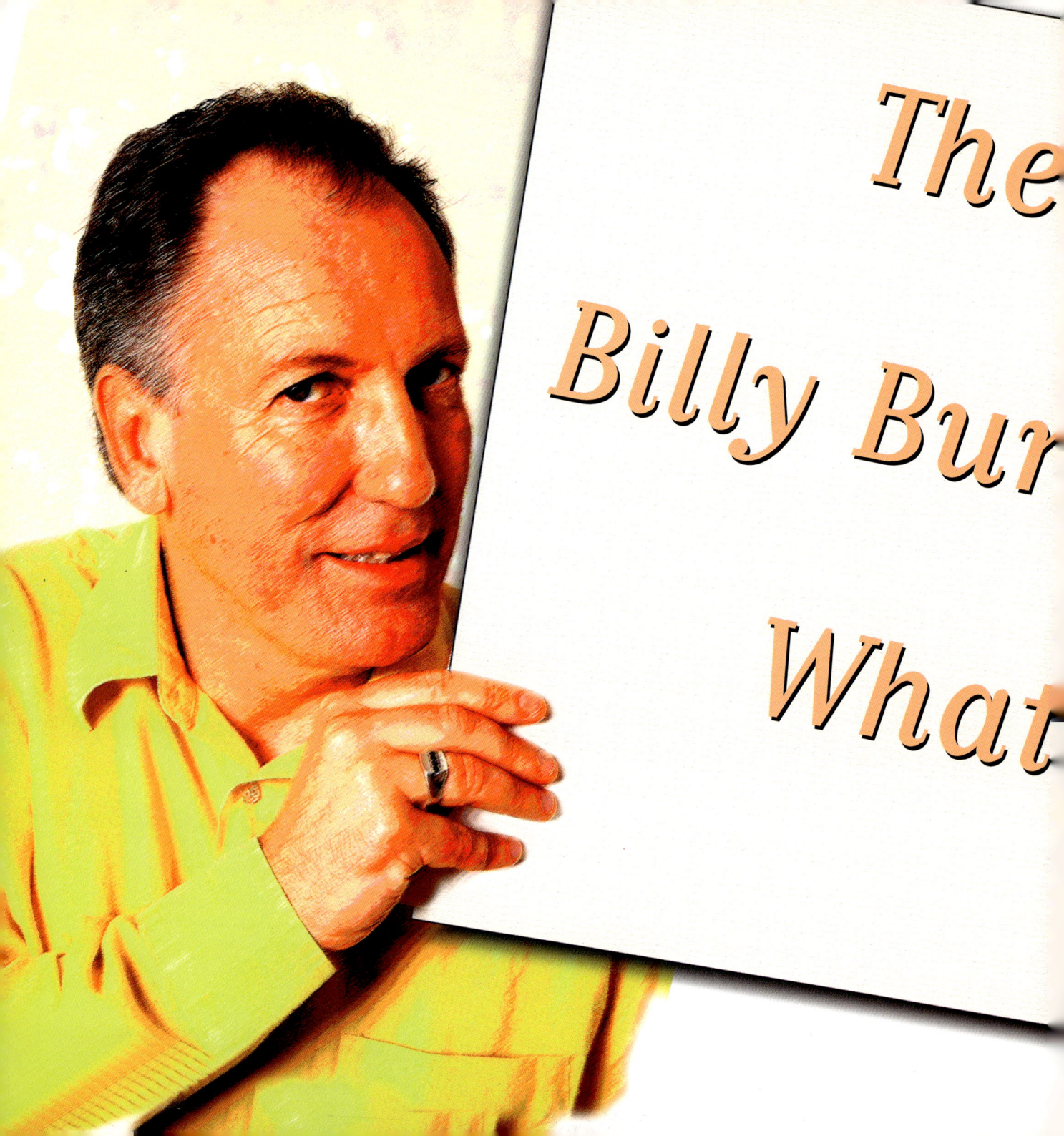

The

Billy Bur

What

Importance of ter: You Are You Read

This magnificent **book**, published by Charles Skilton Ltd of London in 1948, has a beautiful brown hard-cover. I found it when I was about **eight**, in my **grandparents'** (the Mudgeways, of Waterloo Rd, Lower Hutt) bookcase. What a treasure!

"Bad Luck For Bob," "Shirty!", "Sacked!", "Bunter Is Worried". Grand adventures shared by the "chums of the remove". The *Bunter* series were what got me into reading. Yet they were not available through the school library service. Nor were Enid Blyton's stories, *The Famous Five* and *The Secret Seven*.

Educationalists and librarians believed that children exposed to these stories would be exposed to prejudice about race and class structure. Golly may have been a bad influence and questions have been raised about the time Noddy and Big Ears spent in bed together. I, however, never really believed that Bunter's classmate, the "nabob of

Bhanipur", Hurree Jamset Ram Singh, spoke as other Indian people do, when he asked, "But why the puntfulness of the esteemed and ridiculous Bunter?"

Given that what is popular is a matter of fashion (Chorian, the company which owns Enid Blyton's works, had sales last year of £3.7 million), it is to be hoped that a maturing society will allow people to make their own choices.

We are rather fond of rules. Perhaps because they save us from having to make our own decisions.

While staying at a Hamilton hotel recently, I asked for a small bottle of beer in the bottle, so that I could take it into town. The barman said he could not hand me beer in the bottle, that the rules demanded he pour it into a glass. This he did. So I was forced to take the glass downtown, where it sits to this day.

Air New Zealand has some turbo-prop aircraft flying commuter routes, which do not have big enough overhead lockers to accommodate ordinary briefcases. I always carry two on board, contrary to the numerous signs and drawings indicating that you are allowed only one piece of hand baggage.

> *"There is nothing as thrilling as a good book. I have one at my side now."*
>
> – Billy Bunter's Barring-Out by Frank Richards.

Leaving aside the question of what kind of numb-brain would purchase an aircraft with insufficient overhead locker room for its business passengers, there is a reason why I defy the rule. To begin with, I have work to do. This is the age of the word processor, so I need a briefcase on board containing the work – and a word processor with which to write it. In addition, word processors get "fried" in the holds of aircraft and damaged as cargo. No one has solved this problem.

Add to that the intractable problem that the overhead lockers are too small and we have a recipe for disagreement.

Hostesses and stewards ask that I place my hand baggage "under the seat in front of me". That, of course, is where my feet have to go. The safe and comfortable passage of my feet and, indeed, my legs, are part of the hugely expensive ticket price I (or my employers) pay. Strenuous efforts are made nowadays to find me a seat with a vacant seat alongside. It's either that, or the harried hostess finds herself being a personal secretary, having to ferry papers to and from a locker up the front.

There are two ways of looking at my behaviour. One is that I am a grumpy, overbearing prick! The other is that I see clearly that two into one won't go. That rules are so often made for the convenience of the business organisation, bureaucrat or politician, so that the individual's needs come second, third or fourth.

Similarly my ongoing battle over the Palmerston North Airport Company and it's domestic departure tax. I do not and will not pay this charge. It is an abuse of a monopoly situation – a highwayman's tax. I have no other way of getting onto my plane other than through their airport. They imposed a tax on people who are not ratepayers of Palmerston North, who had no vote and no say. (To pay for the new terminal, which I now understand has been paid for, but surprise, surprise – the tax continues to be levied.)

"No taxation without representation" was the cry which led to the War of Independence, when the United States of America broke away from England. I'm not advocating that we break away from Palmerston North because that would leave a huge hole in the map of the North Island with people in

Shannon and Bulls looking nervously over the edge.

But I am a little concerned at the number of people who approach me and say, "Good on ya, Gazza, for not paying that departure tax" – only to see them pay!

We are a nation of people inclined

not to want to make a fuss!

What other country would have allowed their national game to be taken off free-to-air television (apart from those concessions made by Sky) without setting fire to buses and barricading streets?

The Aussies were people brought out in convict ships who have kept themselves fighting fit ever since. They fought against domestic departure taxes in a spectacular manner and I saw some fiery public arguments at airline check-in counters over there. The idea was dropped.

That same trip was the one on which I found myself sitting next to Jock Hobbs as the Cavaliers winged their semi-secret way to South Africa. I said to him, "I hope I never find out you guys are being paid to go there."

I believe I have since found out!

New Zealanders left England quietly, leaving a note for the milkman cancelling the milk. No one noticed we had left until the Christmas cards were returned.

Many Kiwis would see our acquiesence as a virtue, believing that it contributes to peace and harmony. It does not. It makes us prey to the Muldoon type of bullying government and an ingrained belief that not "making a fuss" is the sensible thing to do.

Twelve or more years ago in Gisborne, when banks had not been exposed for their own foolish lending behaviour, then-Labour MP Alan Wallbank drew attention in the *Gisborne Herald* to the plight of a family (parents and three children, as I recall) who were about to have their house auctioned out from around them because the father had bought a truck and was some $20,000 behind on the repayments (he had repaid $110,000).

I talked to the family (who had the backing of their church and were probably as close as you can get to a conscientious, good Christian family) then phoned a number of people I knew. I asked them to attend the auction and back me up because it was my intention to announce that, as the forced sale seemed unreasonable, I would personally urge people not to bid for the house. I was also prepared to move into the house and stay there in an effort to focus media attention onto the issue.

I was horrified to find on the day that only one person I contacted and who expressed concern bothered to turn up.

I was able to focus enough attention on the bank's behaviour that the auction was called off.

The greater shock was the realisation that rather than be seen in a potentially embarrassing situation, friends and associates stayed away.

What would I do for them if they found themselves in the same situation? The fellows of Bunter's remove would have been there!

Maori find this Pakeha unwillingness to stand and be counted a real asset. Given the natural inclination on the marae and in cultural performances to confront ("We will split the head of the Pakeha and drink blood from the skull . . .") we make superb targets!

Filming the East Cape, from Mt Hikurangi to the marae occupied by the curious tribe of Rastafarian-influenced young Maori, provided some interesting moments. The most memorable for me was Friday night in the public bar of the Ruatoria Hotel where a young man advanced on me in a haka, stopping within an inch of my face.

I am not highly schooled in Maori (or, for that matter, Pakeha) etiquette, but I knew enough not to retreat or take my eyes off him. (Later the same night we drank several beers together!)

Pakeha have to understand that Maori politics are likely to be a dramatic business. When the bluffing and posturing starts happening, we must be careful not to fold too soon.

There is more candour and open acknowledgement of problems among the new breed of Maori leadership. MP Dover Samuels talks openly of apathy among Maori in the North and what he sees as the "dial a kaumatua" problem. The criticism of what he refers to as "the Brown Table" by John Tamihere of the Te Whenua O Waipareira Trust in West Auckland is the kind of debate never heard outside the closed shop of Maoridom in the past.

In the end, both Maori and Pakeha have to deal with what are basically the same problems of power and bureaucracy. How to ensure that the wealth and resources in the community are fairly distributed? These problems have to be tackled across the entire community. The Government's own National Health Committee reported in June that more people are becoming ill and are dying because of poverty. Poverty is not the prerogative of one race anymore.

If Pakeha had the same awareness and commitment to their tribal past (and perhaps the same dramatic skills!) as have Maori, not only would there be some very entertaining hui, but the government of the day would be forced to pay attention.

I buy all the old *Bunter*, *Famous Five* and *Secret Seven* books I can find.

By the time I am fifty, I will have a book-lined study with a fireplace and never go outside.

Endword

If you have flicked through this book, you will be aware that mine is a very **tiny mind** indeed.

I don't mean that in any belittling way. There is a virtue, I believe, in bouncing off the walls of your own psyche in public. It helps other people.

Why? Because the truth of the matter is we are all bouncing off the padded (they must be because no one can hear you screaming internally) walls of our brains, or minds, or whatever you choose to call the conscious bit.

Why? Because the mind is a playground full of jungle-gyms, slides and swings.

Why? Because it's free.

When people ask, "Why don't you go overseas?" they often mean, "If you were any

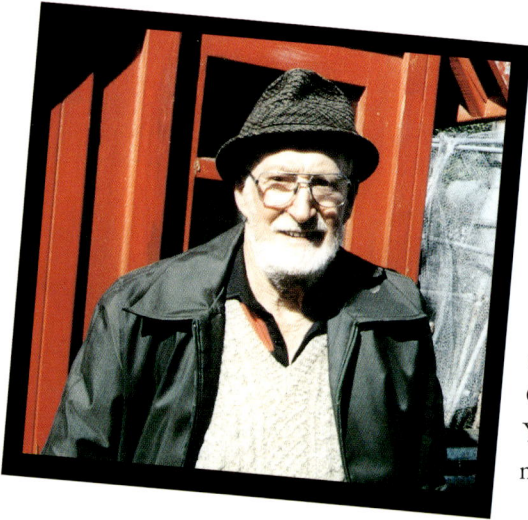

Bill Airey: walked the country and did what we all should do — build a museum to our own lives.

good, you wouldn't be staying here – with us!"

Like Bill Airey, the sprightly gentleman we interviewed on *McCormick* who walked the length of New Zealand in his seventies and has established a museum based around his own life, I find enough to occupy my mind, both in observation and thought, between the back doorstep and the letterbox. Overseas is out of the question, apart from short, sharp excursions. (One encounter in Denver at 2 a.m. with a US Customs officer out of *Fargo* is enough to ruin your life.) You have to make a choice in life – the world, or something more significant.

I do recommend the internal route. Most of the people I have dared to name and draw attention to – writers, actors, cartoonists, "characters" – visit this playground, this park, this familiar neighbourhood in the mind – where they are the only child on the swing.

It is fashionable to dismiss ego (not for long, it's coming back with the Age of the Sovereign Individual) and, certainly, ego used as a bludgeon for such narrow objectives as acquiring personal wealth is lamentable. Lop-sided (in terms of their personal values), egotistical people are horrible to be around.

No, a **fascination** with oneself and one's thought processes is a wonderful basis for a rich and satisfying life.

Personal awareness is not some hocus-pocus, touchy-feely notion. It is the business of putting the eye to the lens. To see the big picture. To make life an epic.

I have rolled to and fro in these pages like a barrel loose in the hold of a ship. You see, I'm doing it again. There are no barrels loose in the holds of ships these days – only huge containers that go overboard and sit just below the waterline waiting for a fishing boat to take down. But in my mind I see wooden ships, barrels, hear the creaking of timber.

The economy (named Belinda) we have decided is not worth worrying about. The mathematics are such that the poor get 28 cents worth of tax cuts and the reasonably well-to-do over ten times that. You can only give tax cuts, a representative of the Round Table said, to those who pay tax.

Quite right! Hear, hear!

Do as the Italians and the French (according to Kim Hill) do – drink more red wine and forget about her (Belinda – not Kim).

The business of business is just another game. Those whose range of interests is focused in that direction have got it all sewn up. If you think you want to break in, you've got to learn the codes, preferably have testicles, understand the notion of a hierarchy, go to absurd lengths to be nice to people you have no earthly reason to admire.

It is all too much for the average human being.

Likewise, as explained, being a sports hero requires all kind of sacrifices of logic and better judgment. Even at the top and with a Spice Girl in tow – like Britain's highest-paid soccer player, David Beckham – you can still retaliate against an Argentinian and get sent off, costing your country the game.

Then, like movie stars and politicians, you get the universal finger of media scorn pointed at you.

At the end of the day, it's David sitting on the edge of the bed next to whichever Spice it is, head in hands, saying, "Why, why, why?"

Remember that scene. Not just him and her but the drawers in the hotel bedroom which have never been opened, the little fridge humming away, the coathangers attached to the bar in the wardrobe . . .

Is there not a universal sense of sorrow?

The first half of life is about pushing the envelope – of discovery and conquest, of saying "Hi there!" and "What will yours be?"

The second half of life (for the worldly wise) requires a quick flit out to the deck, the folding of deck chairs and a shifting of pot plants out of the wind. There is a storm coming. It's time to close the French doors.

Well done, Mother!

As the light fades, the last of it on strong forearms rising out of the foam in the sink, let us say out loud:

This is the way
my life ends
Not with a bang
But in my jumper.